NOW AND FOREVER—LET'S MAKE LOVE

Also by Joan Elizabeth Lloyd

NICE COUPLES DO

IF IT FEELS GOOD

COME PLAY WITH ME

BEDTIME STORIES FOR LOVERS

BLACK SATIN

THE PLEASURES OF JESSICA LYNN

SLOW DANCING

Now and Forever— Let's Make Love

From first kiss to fiftieth anniversary...making sex hot at every stage of your life

JOAN ELIZABETH LLOYD

WARNER BOOKS

A Time Warner Company

Warner Books, Inc., 1271 Avenue of the Americas, New York, NY 10020
Visit our Web site at http://warnerbooks.com

 A Time Warner Company

ISBN 1-56865-560-6

Printed in the United States of America

Book design and composition by L&G McRee
Jacket design by Rachel McClain

*This book is dedicated, as always, to Ed,
now and forever. Together, we make life fun,
in and out of the bedroom.*

*I would like to thank my son-in-law, John Petty,
who is the author of four of the "Ageless Fantasies":
Jeff's, Ted's, Melissa's, and Dave's. I'm sure you
will find they are a valuable addition to this work,
and I use them happily with his permission.*

CONTENTS

Now and Forever—
Let's Make

LOVE

1 ❧
How to Make It Happen

BRAD AND AMY'S STORY

*T*hey left their condo at sunset. Brad had his brightly colored towel draped around his neck; Amy had hers tied around her waist. As they approached the path through the low, stunted scrub, they dropped their joined hands and made their way single file to the beach, which was still warm from the day's heat. Without words, they kicked off their shoes and wandered down to the line between the waves and the sand. They stood for a moment and watched gulls wheel through the cooling air and dive between the whitecaps. Sandpipers raced back and forth just in front of the breaking waves. The air smelled of sea and salt.

"I love this time of day," Amy said, tucking a strand of hair behind her ear.

"Me, too." Brad took her hand and they walked along the hard-packed sand in silence. The sun painted the sky amazing shades of pink, orange, and deep purple over the deepening blue. Brad stopped, turned Amy toward him, and cupped her face with his large hands. "Amy, I love you so much, I don't even want to consider spending the rest of my life without you. I've been thinking about this a lot and . . . well, will you marry me?"

Amy was flabbergasted. She and Brad had lived together for seven months, and she hadn't been sure that he was interested in making their arrangement official. "I never thought . . ."

"I know," Brad said. "I guess I didn't either until recently. But I want the world to know that we're going to spend the rest of our lives together." When Amy hesitated, Brad added, "I know it's complicated, but it will all work out. I love you and want to marry you. That's all that's important. Do you love me?"

"Oh Brad," she said, "you know I love you with all my heart."

"Then marry me."

Slowly, a smile spread over Amy's face. "I very much want to marry you."

Brad caught his breath, not daring to hope. "You mean that? You will?"

Amy laughed out loud with the sheer joy of it. "Yes, I will."

Brad grabbed Amy around the waist, lifted her bare feet off the sand, and swung her around. "Oh babe, that's sensational." He lowered her, sliding her against his body, feeling the length of her against the length of him. He set her feet down, leaned over, and pressed his mouth on hers. He tangled his fingers in her dark hair and massaged her scalp, changing the position of his mouth to taste every bit of Amy's. "I love you so."

Amy slid her arms up Brad's chest and placed one hand on each side of his face, relishing the taste and feel of him.

Brad looked each way along the beach and saw no one else on the sand. Without much thought, he grabbed the bottom of Amy's T-shirt and pulled it up over her head. Noticing the surprised look on Amy's face, Brad said, "There's no one but us anywhere, and it's almost dark. What better way is there to celebrate?"

Amy quickly looked around the deserted beach, smiled shyly, then nodded. Brad took the towel from around his neck and spread it just beyond the water-line, then spread hers beside it. He quickly pulled off his clothes and then unfastened Amy's bra and removed her shorts and panties. He eased her down onto the towel, then settled beside her.

He gazed down at her naked body, barely visible in the fading light. She was tiny and soft, with ample hips, a slight stomach, and small, soft breasts. "So beautiful," he whispered, running the palm of his hand over the body that was so familiar yet ever new. He lightly pinched one nipple and watched it tighten. He was suddenly overwhelmed with his hunger for her.

He suckled at her breast while sliding a hand to the curly hair between her thighs. She was damp, ready for him. "I want to make love to you very slowly," Brad said, "but I'm suddenly so hungry." He reached into the pocket of his shorts, which were lying on the warm sand beside him, unwrapped a condom, and unrolled it on his hard penis.

As he crouched between Amy's spread legs, he felt her hand slide down his hairy chest and across his belly to grasp his hard cock. She squeezed gently, then raised her knees slightly and placed the tip of his hardness against her open pussy. "Do it, darling," she whispered. "Yes, do it."

She raised her hips, and he felt his cock slide slowly into her hot, moist channel. He was so hungry that it was only moments before he lost control. "Baby," he screamed, feeling Amy's body meet his, stroke for stroke. "Oh God." He erupted deep inside of Amy's body. Amy wrapped her legs around Brad's waist and held him against her for a long time.

As his body slowly relaxed, he felt the cool water lap against the soles of his feet. "Baby," he said breathlessly, "you didn't come."

"Later, when you're feeling refreshed," she said, giggling, "we'll see whether you can make up for that lapse."

"You'll really marry me?" he asked again, wiggling his toes in the spume.

"Yes. I want to, you know that. But it will create so many problems."

"I know. We'll have to figure out the Social Security. And telling your children and mine will be quite a job. They'll never understand."

"Oh Lord," Amy said, slipping back into her clothes. "Do you realize that we'll be getting married in the same year that I become a grandmother for the first time?"

Brad finished dressing, picked up his towel, and ran his fingers through his iron-gray hair. Then he took Amy's hand and laughed out loud. "God, I love you, Grandma."

"And I love you, too, you old fart." Hand in hand, they walked through the darkness toward their apartment.

● ● ●

Life has changed dramatically over the last thirty years, and the sound you are hearing right now is the gentle pop of myths exploding, myths we will be discussing at length in this book.

Most couples who are making the decision to commit to each other are in their twenties or thirties. Pop. Couples nearing and past retirement age, like Brad and Amy in the story you just read, and my partner, Ed, and I, are pledging to spend the rest of their lives together. Of course, Social Security and other marriage penalties frequently make living together more feasible than marriage, but the depth of the commitment is no less.

Most of those making the decision to be together are doing it for the first time, and that commitment will last forever. Pop. Fewer than half are making that decision for the first time. Sadly, divorce is rampant. You can't pick up a magazine without reading an article about starting over.

Brad and Amy's story illustrates a few more inaccurate but deeply held beliefs:

Quickies are bad. Pop. Quickies, like the one Brad and Amy just had, can be wonderful. So can long lovemaking sessions that last hours. But variety is the spice of a relationship. Sometimes quickies are hot, hungry, and deliciously satisfying. At other times, longies are just what the doctor ordered.

The sex drive slows during your forties and fifties, then stops altogether. Pop. Pop. Pop. Boom! The idea that sex drive inevitably decreases in the middle years is baloney. Sometimes there is a physiological reason for a lack of interest, due to disease or medication. All too often, however, the decrease in sexual frequency is due to other problems that couples don't feel the need to resolve because, they say, "We're too old for that stuff, anyway."

Condoms spoil good sex. It's like taking a shower in a raincoat. Pop. Condoms are necessary in this age of AIDS and other sexually transmitted diseases. Any two people, even Brad and Amy in our story, who haven't been either celibate or exclusive for at least five years, need to protect themselves from the spread of such diseases. And condoms, when made a routine part of sex play, don't spoil the fun. Although Ed and I have been together for more than ten years, we still use a condom occasionally, and the feeling of that cold, lubricated latex is, for me, exciting and fun. And putting a condom on can be foreplay in and of itself.

Women need to achieve orgasm to be satisfied with a sexual encounter. Pop. Not so. Lovemaking is close-ness, sharing, peaks and valleys of sensation and excitement. It can frequently be impossible to know where your personal pleasure leaves off and the plea-sure that your partner is experiencing begins. I some-times find that Ed's orgasm can satisfy me, as Brad's did for Amy. Of course, at other times I initiate sex play after Ed's orgasm, and my climax can be extreme-ly satisfying. Sometimes I climax before he does.

Although this story doesn't illustrate the next few myths, here are some that are worth exploding.

Men are always hard, eager, and anxious for sex. Pop. So many of the women with whom I've spoken, either in person or via letters, have told me that their male partner isn't interested in sex more than once or twice a month. If that satisfies both parties, fine. Fortunately, the FDA hasn't established a minimum or maximum requirement for intercourse. (Don't smile—it might happen yet.) Whatever satisfies both partners is the correct amount. However, there are many women who are interested in having sex more often than are the men in their life, and vice versa. This situation can be remedied, to some extent, but it requires some thought and preparation.

Nice comfortable sex is best. Experimentation, especially with off-center stuff, is not for ordinary people like me; kinky sex is for kinky people. Pop. It's true that what is comfortable is nice. But there are pleasures you've previously only dreamt about that are possible between you and your partner. The new and unusual is exciting at any stage of a relationship. Anything that's enjoyed by both partners is good for them. Anything not enjoyed by both is not. Period. And there's so much you've probably never explored.

Men get hot very fast and women warm up slowly. No, don't explode that one. Although, like all generalities, it does have exceptions, this one's true most of the time. I heard a wonderful quote recently: "Men flame like a match; women heat like an iron." This is very true, and it's a situation that's often underestimated. Find a compromise, the books and articles say simplistically. He needs to slow down; she needs to try to speed up her reactions. Sure. So much more easily said than done. But there are ways.

Why do I bring up all these dearly held beliefs? Because together, through the next two hundred pages or so, we're going to look at mistaken beliefs about lovemaking. We'll search for truths, solutions, and for the fun that's to be had between partners, from those who are new to each other to those who've been together since the Eisenhower administration and longer.

Together, we're going to investigate exciting ways

to make lovemaking, at all stages of a relationship, hot, new, and fun.

Before we begin, there are several topics that need to be addressed. First, and most important, no section of this book is specific to one stage of life or another. Of course, there are problems that affect those at one stage of a relationship more than at another: dealing with small children, the problems of aging, the good news and bad news about new relationships. But the suggestions for activities to relieve some of the sexual tensions that go with these problems and the ideas for spicing up a sex life are generic. All ages can benefit from lengthening foreplay, from using all the senses to bring out new feelings, from ideas for new activities, and from suggestions to facilitate communication between partners.

Although I encourage you to skip around, there is something in every chapter for everyone, so don't decide that because you're twenty-seven years old and you and your partner have a two-year-old son the chapter titled "The Empty Nest" has nothing of value for you.

You can read this book from cover to cover if you like, or you can begin with the section that seems to apply to your relationship, then skip around later. There are new ideas everywhere, so just keep an open mind as you read.

This book is also filled with short stories about ordinary people having fun in the bedroom, on the grass, at a motel bar, or in an elevator. They will engage in some activities that you and your partner may want to experiment with, some that are fun to fantasize about but that you wouldn't think of actually doing, and some that are just "not your thing." Not everything is for everyone.

You will notice that few of the people in the stories are described in detail and that I've given the characters plain vanilla names. I hope that you can imagine yourself and your partner in one or more of those situations. Think of them as people like yourselves, doing things you've always wanted to do. Should you decide to read one or more of these stories aloud, you can personalize the tale by changing the names of the characters and describing them as if they were you and your partner.

In addition to problems, suggestions, and stories, each chapter contains a section called "Try Something New." These sections contain stories and useful information about a new activity: storytelling, cybersex, browsing through catalogs, and playing out power fantasies. I included one in each chapter, but none is specific to an age or a particular stage of a relationship, because there is no age limit on anything you want to try. If you think it might feel good, go for it.

At the end of each chapter, you'll find a section titled "Ageless Fantasies," adventurous tales of delicious interludes, each story demonstrating how dreams can come true.

Keep an open mind. I've said it before and I'll say it again through the book. It's an important phrase. I'm going to discuss ideas that may seem "bad" to you. I will certainly admit that not all sexual activities are for everyone. Many of you may have no interest in being tied to the bed or in making love on the dining room table. But that doesn't mean these are "bad" ideas. They are just not your thing. Maybe you've never ventured far from the beaten path. That's fine, too. But don't label ideas as "good" or "bad." Either they suit your taste or they don't. And take care never to label your partner as "bad" for suggesting something off-center. The idea may not appeal to you, but your partner has been very brave to suggest it.

Try not to make your "sounds good" versus "let's not" decisions based on what you're *supposed* to like or dislike, what nice girls or good guys *should* do or not do.

Let's take oral sex, for example. The new Kinsey Institute report states: "Although various studies show that 50 to 80 percent of women perform fellatio, only 35 to 65 percent of those find it to be pleasurable; the rest are indifferent (that is, they can take it or leave it) or do not enjoy it at all."

What was your first reaction as you read that? Did you think what most of us do when reading sexual statistics?

Am I in the majority? Yes! Phew. I'm okay.

Or: No! I must be weird. I'm in the minority. Something's wrong with me.

I have a wonderful mental picture of a woman reading the latest study on sexual activities aloud to her husband of forty years. "Dear," she says, her lower lip quivering, "it says here that only five percent of Americans enjoy making love standing on their heads."

"Oh darling," he answers, "I never realized that we were doing something so kinky. I guess that means we have to stop."

"And after all these years," she moans.

"Maybe we can do it one last time," he suggests, winking at her.

"Well maybe," she says, grinning.

Point made? It really is pretty silly to judge the things that you and your partner enjoy by other people's standards. If it feels good and you both get pleasure, do it.

Very little that I will say in *Now and Forever* is gender-specific. Both men and women have fantasies. Both men and women are occasionally discontented with their sex lives. Both men and women enjoy telling dirty stories or playing with sex toys.

Now let's consider the awkward problem I have with pronouns. If I put "him/her" or "she/he" in every appropriate place, this book would be both hard to type and cumbersome to read. Therefore, I will use my pronouns randomly. I will just choose the gender that most people think the situation might apply to.

A suggestion: Let's say you've read something in this book—or any book, for that matter—that ignites a spark in your mind. Or perhaps you find your pulse racing and you think what a couple did in a particular story sounds wonderful. They made love in his office—right on the desk—while the cleaning crew was in the next room. You take a deep breath; your knees quiver and your heart pounds. I'd love to be that brave, that free, that hot, you think.

Then you think some more. Maybe Charlie (or Charlene) wouldn't like it. Maybe my husband will think I'm weird for even suggesting it. Then you remember how he reacted the last time you suggested something unusual, the funny look in his eyes, the subtle but, to you, obvious change in his body language.

Maybe my wife will reject me for even considering such a thing. She'll decide that something's wrong with our marriage. She'll think I'm getting ideas because I'm having an affair.

No, you decide, you won't mention it.

That night, sex is particularly stimulating because you're picturing the office with the lights out and the sounds of vacuuming in the next room. You make love with new vigor, new enthusiasm.

That's not all bad. Anything that leads to an evening of good sex is great. But what if you could mention your idea to your partner and give him time to digest the idea and consider that it might be fun to try. There's a special delight when you introduce someone you care about to something that becomes a special favorite, sexual or not. I convinced Ed to try sushi for the first time and he got me to eat boiled peanuts, and both of us are better for that. New pleasures. But how? I've got an easy way for you to do that; I call it book-marking.

Here's how it works. Let's say you find an arousing idea or a story about a couple making love in an excit-ing new way. Slip a bookmark into the book at the page where that new idea is mentioned. Put a second bookmark where a couple acts out the fantasy you would like to try, so your lover will understand what you're doing.

Then put the book under your husband's pillow, or in your wife's briefcase. Give him time to read a bit and understand that you're suggesting something won-derful—something new and a little scary, but wonder-ful. No, it's not the specific idea that's wonderful. What is wonderful is that you're suggesting to him that you two try something different.

"Honey," you might say, "this is an interesting book. I'd love it if you'd read a bit. There are two book-marks. Why don't you take a look at the sections I've selected?"

I think it's fantastically brave and loving. You're saying to your partner, Hey, I want to play with you. I don't want merely to fantasize anymore. I don't want to play with anyone else. I want to play with you because I love you and because I think we can both have fun with this.

Risky? Yes. But the risk carries a great reward.

What will he think when he begins to read? First will come the knee-jerk reaction. What's the matter— what we have isn't good enough? Where does she learn this stuff—from those silly women's magazines? She's a nice woman and can't possibly be interested in that. Is she really saying she wants to try something kinky?

Then he'll check to see where you've put your second bookmark. He'll flip the pages and read. Nah, he'll think, she can't mean this. Can she? Would she?

There can be two possible outcomes. The best would be that he realizes this is an idea he's been thinking about, too. Holy shit, he thinks, she really wants to do this? He's delighted, excited, and, literally or figuratively, drags you off into the bedroom and . . . Well, you understand.

However, there is another possibility. Oh Lord, he thinks. She can't want to do *that*. It's sick, crazy, weird. How can I tell her that this turns me off totally?

How indeed? Remember that your partner has taken a great risk and shared her innermost fantasy with you. She has told you something wonderful and opened a dialogue by saying, Let's play together. Well, isn't there something that you've always wanted to try that you've never had the courage to share? I'll bet there is. Aren't you lucky that she took the risk first! Now you have the opportunity to share your desires, as well.

What to do? Mellow out and relax. Read through

other sections of this book and move the bookmark to a story that makes you hot. Then return the book to your partner. How many times you move the bookmark is irrelevant. What's important is that you're communicating. You're exploring things that might be fun, and eventually you will find one that gets both of you excited. Then go ravish each other. Do it. It's all fun, as long as each of you gives and receives pleasure from the activity.

When you find something new and erotically exciting, go for it. You might get yourself into a silly situation that neither of you had anticipated. Okay, giggle. You might decide that something that sounded like a great idea turned out to be a lousy one. Say so.

If it's wonderful, be encouraging. Purr, moan, say "That feels so good," or "Move your hand over here a little bit." Afterward, tell each other "That was terrific," or say "That didn't turn out quite the way I'd expected." Communicate—out loud. This is all new and scary, but you're together, and that makes so much possible.

Now let's begin our journey into the realms of creative lovemaking and see what problems, solutions, suggestions, and new ideas are out there for a couple who has the courage to try.

2.
Newly Partnered

> *Three boys—one English, one Italian, and one French—accidentally peeked into a motel window and saw a couple on their honeymoon bouncing around on the bed.*
>
> *The English boy jumped back and said, "They're fighting."*
>
> *The Italian boy looked at him incredulously. "You don't know anything," he said. "They're making love."*
>
> *The French boy smiled softly. "Yes, they are. And badly, too."*

You've made the big decision. You and your partner are exclusive. Whether you've just gotten married or have recently moved in together, you're committed. It's a wonderful time, a time of exploration, a time of new discoveries about each other, a time of new adventures and new problems.

While you were dating, seeing each other a few

times a week at best, you were hot for each other. You anticipated each meeting for hours, even days, being sure you looked your best, smelled your best, sounded your best. You dressed carefully, put on your best cologne, and jumped into bed whenever you had the time and the place. The time might have been during your lunch hour and the place might have been the backseat of your car in the parking lot, but you found time to be together. It was wonderful.

Now things are a bit different. You're together every evening, every night. You go to sleep together and wake up together. You see him floss his teeth. He smells your morning breath. You see each other's naked bodies before bed every night. By itself, that sight isn't as stimulating as it used to be. Understandably, frequency cools the flames a bit. The urgency is gone, and there's nothing wrong with that. It's a natural part of getting to know each other. But many couples worry if the frequency drops from once a day to once or twice a week.

More than thirty-five years ago, before my seventeen-year marriage, my then boyfriend and I learned about sex together. We made love anywhere we could, from the front seat of his 1954 Ford to my living-room couch. What began with kissing escalated to petting, caressing, and mutual masturbation. We were, and had been, each other's one and only, and we were hot together. By the time we were actually ready to remove our clothes and "do it," we were so excited that our mating was fast and, although not orgasmic for me, satisfying. We made love anytime, anyplace we could.

Once we were married, however, I subtly set a few limitations. First, I limited our couplings to soft, comfortable surfaces. No more gearshift levers in awkward places, no rug burns from living-room floors, no scratchy sofa cushions. I wanted a bed. Next, I told my husband that I did not like lovemaking while I was menstruating. Many men and women find that there is no reason not to continue intercourse at those times, but it didn't feel good to me, and it still doesn't. So once sex was possible every evening if we wanted, I could suggest a few restrictions. My husband probably had his limits, too, but we never really discussed them. They just got subtly integrated into the pattern of our loving.

As a newlywed and a product of the sexually naïve society of the fifties, I was uneducated as to what to expect from a sexual relationship. The fact that I had never climaxed didn't faze me. If the truth be told, I'm not sure I knew what an orgasm was until I had been married for more than ten years. However, what I didn't know didn't bother me.

Nowadays, women are, I hope, much more attuned to their own needs, both physical and emotional. Many women have explored their own sexuality with a number of partners, each learning and teaching the other, exploring the things that give pleasure. Although there are those who still, sadly, label masturbation "bad," many women have learned about their own bodies by touching themselves—a fine art, which, unfortunately, I didn't explore until after my thirtieth birthday.

As a woman, if you don't already know your body and its pleasure and "hot buttons," this might be a good time to learn, the way Sandy did.

SANDY'S STORY

Sandy lay in the bathtub, reading her newest romance novel. "He slipped his fingers between her legs," she read, "and caressed her wet flesh. He felt her hips move as though they had a mind of their own. 'Oh yes, my love,' he crooned, 'want me. I'll give you so much pleasure. . . .'"

Sandy's eyes moved to the ceiling. Although she was nineteen, she had never really explored her own body. She had had intercourse many times over the past year with a few different boys in her classes at the local community college, and those times had been exciting and wonderful. But, she thought now, no one has ever slipped his fingers into my naked folds. How would it feel? she wondered.

Holding the book in one hand and rereading the last few sentences, she slipped the index finger of her other hand through her pubic hair and between her outer lips. This feels so slutty and dirty, she thought. But it also feels different. Her finger gently rubbed through the folds on either side of her swelling clitoris.

As her inquisitive finger slid farther back, she found her inner lips and the slippery substance oozing from inside her. "Ummm," she heard herself purr. She gradually began to explore, touching places that she had never touched before, enjoying the pleasure of it. I never realized how nice this would feel, she thought. She slowly realized that her nipples were hardening and she was getting hungry. I want something inside my pussy, she realized. She looked around and saw her toothbrush in the glass beside the sink. I wonder . . .

She reached for the brush and then hesitated. I can't do this, she thought. It's kinky and perverse. But, she argued, it's my body, and I can do with it what I want. And I want this.

She took the toothbrush and lowered it into the warm water. She slid the handle through the folds she had so recently explored for the first time with her finger. Her breathing faster now, she tentatively inserted the smooth plastic handle of the toothbrush into her slippery pussy. Marveling at the difference in feel between the water and her own juices, she rubbed the handle over her wet membranes. She lowered her dry hand into the water and rubbed her now-swollen clitoris. She found places that felt exceptionally good and then rubbed them more, until she felt the shudders of a small orgasm tremble through her body.

"Oh my," she said later as she tossed the toothbrush into the sink. "Oh my."

It is easy for a man to discover exactly what excites him. He usually explores his body and finds his erogenous zones at an early age. They're so easy to find. They just stick out there in plain sight and within easy reach. Psychologists believe that every boy masturbates frequently before he reaches puberty, whether with a hand, while lying on his stomach on the floor, or while rubbing against a favorite toy. After puberty, hormones rage and erections are sudden and often unexpected. Many a teenaged boy has had to ride past his bus stop to avoid standing up and revealing his immense hard-on.

But here again, society makes things difficult.

"Don't touch that; it's dirty."

"You'll grow hair on your hands."

"You'll become desensitized, so you won't be able to enjoy a woman."

There are even parents who tell their sons, "You have only so many erections. Keep doing that and you'll use them up. Then what?" Many men who've internalized this warning think that by age fifty they will be unable to have an erection—something that they believe is borne out by the natural changes that come with age, and which I will cover in chapter 5.

So we make a man ashamed and afraid of touching his own body. He will probably do it anyway, although he may become frustrated while desire wars with societal warnings.

As a society, we really mess with our children's heads.

Eventually, with hormones rampant, young people begin to experiment with sex. They touch each other, rub, and finally try sexual intercourse. It's wonderful and fulfilling, and soon everything else slips into the background. All they can think about is their next opportunity to be together, maybe with the time, the place, and the privacy to have intercourse. It's probably not lovemaking yet, just acrobatic fucking, but it's very satisfying.

The first step in establishing a mutually satisfying relationship is to know your own body. If you don't, explore. After all, how can you help your partner learn what gives you pleasure if you haven't found out yourself?

You and your partner have made the commitment to be a couple, but the animal heat has cooled a bit. Make that the good news. Now that you're partners and have the time to learn and share, maybe the two of you can take this opportunity to learn not only about yourself but also about each other and what gives pleasure and what does not. In the story that follows, we meet up with Sandy a few years later. Although by now, Sandy has learned what pleases her body, discussing specific sexual matters with her new husband, Jake, isn't always easy.

SANDY AND JAKE'S STORY

Sandy and Jake had met at an intersection when, as the result of a drunken driver, both Sandy's Toyota and Jake's Escort had been damaged. As they exchanged information, Jake had looked into Sandy's deep brown eyes and suggested that they wait for the tow trucks in the diner just down the block. Coffee led to dinner, and seven months later, they were married.

About six weeks after the wedding, Sandy and Jake were lying in bed together, watching the evening news. "I'm finding it hard to come down after the awful day I had. I think I'll take a bath," Sandy said.

Playfully, Jake asked, "Can I join you?"

"There's not a lot of room in the tub," Sandy said, smiling seductively and knowing that playing with her new husband was just the tonic she needed.

"That's the idea," Jake said, and soon they were naked and up to their chests in hot, soapy water.

"Is your leg comfortable?" Sandy asked as she shifted position.

Jake wiggled his toes, which were firmly pressed against Sandy's hip. "Fine," he said, taking the soap from the holder and working up a thick lather in his hands. "Let me wash your shoulders." He rubbed his slippery hands over Sandy's neck and upper arms, then down her breasts.

"Ooh baby," Sandy said, "we won't get much washing done if you keep that up."

"I'm keeping it up, okay?" Jake said, swirling his soapy fingers over Sandy's wet breast. "Feel." While massaging one globe, Jake took Sandy's hand and guided it between his legs to his hard cock.

"You certainly are up," Sandy said, grinning. Jake was always hot for her, and she lusted after him, as well.

"Do you like the way my hand feels?" Jake asked on the spur of the moment.

"Of course," Sandy said, enjoying the feel of Jake's fingers on her breast and her hand wrapped around his cock.

Jake slid his hand lower and rubbed Sandy's belly. It was all Sandy could do not to pull away as Jake found her most ticklish spots. "You don't really like where I'm touching you now, do you?" Jake persisted.

"It's just that I'm ticklish," Sandy admitted, and she felt Jake's hand stop.

"You don't like being tickled, do you?"

"Not really."

"So why don't you just tell me to stop? Or move my hand?"

Sandy hesitated. "It's hard to tell you I don't like something you do."

"But how else am I supposed to know? I want to do things that give you pleasure, not things that make you uncomfortable."

"I know that, silly," Sandy said.

"But how can I do that if you don't tell me what you like, or at least what you don't like? I'm not a mind reader, you know."

When Sandy had no answer, Jake slipped his fingers into Sandy's pussy hair. "Do you like it when I do this?" he asked. "I really want to touch you in all the best places."

"What you're doing feels good," Sandy said, sighing.

"Yes," Jake persisted, "but what feels best?"

"I don't know. Just touch me." To deflect the embarrassing conversation, Sandy rubbed her hand along Jake's cock. "Maybe we should get out of the tub and make love."

"Hmm, maybe we should." Jake stood up, guided Sandy to a standing position, opened the drain, and turned on the shower. "But first, I, for one, need to rinse off," he said, adjusting the shower to a warm pulsating spray.

Sandy felt Jake turn her so her back was against his chest, her chest directly under the water. He wrapped his hands around her and massaged her breasts, pinching her hard nipples until they stood out from her chest, tight and tingling. "Nice," she purred.

As the water sluiced down her body, Sandy felt Jake's teeth nibble at the tendon that ran across the top of her shoulder. "I don't want to tickle you," he said as his hand slid quickly down her belly and between her legs. "Does this tickle?"

"No, baby," Sandy said. "That feels great."

His fingers rubbed her erect clit. "Does this feel better?"

"Feels good," Sandy moaned.

"Yes, but what feels best?"

"You do. Everything you do." Sandy was breathing quickly now, hungry for what was to come.

"Show me," Jake said. "Put your hand over mine and show me where you want me to touch you."

Sandy stiffened. She frequently masturbated in the warm water of the tub, but this was entirely different. This was kinky. She couldn't touch herself with anyone knowing—even Jake, even with his hand between her hand and her body. "Oh baby. Everything you do gives me pleasure," she mumbled. "You know that."

"I do, but I want to know more."

"You are very stubborn," Sandy said, her reluctance cooling some of her sexual desire. "Can't you let this go?"

"I don't want to, baby," Jake said. "I want to know how to please you."

Seizing on a way to divert his attention, Sandy said, "Will you show me what you like?"

Jake hesitated, then said softly, "Okay. I will if you will." He quickly turned off the shower, grabbed two towels, and handed one to his wife.

In only moments, naked and still damp from their shower, Sandy and Jake were in the bedroom, stretched out on the bed. Jake's hand caressed her breast, teasing her erect nipple, his mouth beside her ear. "Show me what you like, baby."

"You promised you'd show me what *you* like first." She propped herself up on her elbow, both excited and curious.

Jake smiled up at her. "I guess I did." His cock was hard and it stuck straight up from his groin. He took Sandy's hand in his and molded her fingers around his hard shaft. He slowly used Sandy's fist to rub up and down. "I like it when you hold my cock like this."

Sandy had rubbed Jake's cock often, so she reached for the tube of K-Y jelly on the bedside table. "Let me make my hand slippery," she said, squeezing a big dollop of chilling lubricant onto her palm. "Okay," she said, placing the tube back in the drawer, "where were we?"

"You had your hand on my cock," Jake said, his breathing raspy and uneven.

"And you were showing me what you like."

Again, Jake took Sandy's hand and pressed it against his erection. "Cold," he said. "I love it when your hand is so cold and so slippery." He slowly guided her hand up and down his cock.

He's moving much more slowly than I do, she thought, and pressing more softly. I always thought he liked it fast and tight.

He guided her hand to his balls and tickled the sac with the tips of her fingers.

Sandy looked down at her husband's closed eyes and the look of pure joy on his face. She felt him shudder. "Should I rub more?" she asked.

"Yes," he groaned. "And touch here." He pushed her finger to the small area of skin between the base of his balls and his anus. "Stroke here, softly." His breathing quickened.

Sandy used her free hand to surround his slippery cock while massaging his balls and skin with the other. "This way? Does it feel good?"

"So good that you're driving me crazy." Jake's back arched with need, and sweat broke out on his forehead.

Sandy was amazed. She had never imagined she could give so much pleasure with just her hands. She had used her mouth on Jake's cock from time to time, but this was new. "Could you actually come from me touching you like this?"

"Continue and you'll know soon enough," he panted.

Sandy was thrilled as she watched his jaw clench. She rubbed and massaged, watching Jake's face to see what gave the most pleasure. Soon she felt his cock start to twitch and spasm. "I'm going to come, baby," he moaned. "Stop right now if you don't want me to come yet."

"Oh baby. I'd love to watch you come," Sandy said. "Faster?"

"Yes. Faster. Now." Jake came, streams of thick, sticky fluid spurting from his cock.

A short time later, Jake had recovered enough to remember the second part of their bargain. He snuggled against Sandy, his tongue circling her ear. "Please," Jake said, resting his hand on her mound. "Now show me how to touch you. You're so wet and so hot, I know you want me."

"Yes, I do want you. Very much. I want you to make love to me."

Jake looked down at his flaccid cock. "Not a chance for a while," he said. "Anyway, we had a deal. I want to learn about you—about your body." He moved so his mouth was above Sandy's right breast. Then he licked from her breastbone to her areola, not touching her nipple. Again and again, he licked, avoiding the erect nub he knew she wanted him to touch. "Do you want me to lick your nipple?"

"Yes," Sandy whispered.

Jake nipped at her erect flesh. "Like that?"

"Oh yes." Jake teased Sandy's breast until the nipple was hard; then he switched to the other one. As her hips began to move, Sandy felt her hunger increase. "Love me."

"You'll have to show me what you want," Jake said simply.

"Please. Touch me."

"No, baby." He lifted her hand, placed it on her lower belly, then placed his on top. "Show me. Touch yourself while I feel what you like." Jake knew Sandy was reluctant, despite what they had just done, but he insisted. "Do it." Jake's voice took on the commanding quality that Sandy found very erotic. "Do it for me."

Slowly, Sandy slid her hand lower, with Jake's hand resting gently on top of it.

"Yes, baby," Jake whispered. "Do it for me."

Sandy slipped her fingers into her folds and felt her clit, so hard and needy. Her fingers knew just what she needed, but she was reluctant to reveal how well she knew her own body.

"Right here?" Jake whispered, his breath cool on her wet breast.

"Yes."

"And here?"

"Oh yes."

No longer able to resist the pull of her own body and the insistence in Jake's voice, Sandy surrendered to her own needs. Her fingers found the places she liked to be touched and she rubbed them. "Yes, baby," she heard Jake whisper. "Oh yes. That's so good. Make it feel good."

As she rubbed, Jake's fingers slipped inside her, first one and then another, until her pussy was filled with him. It had never felt like this before, her masturbating while her husband's fingers rubbed and stretched her. Higher and higher she drove herself, until she felt the familiar tension begin low in her belly. "Yes," she said through gritted teeth. "Yes."

She knew Jake had moved so he could watch their hands, but she no longer cared about anything but her approaching climax. "Don't stop," she begged him as his hand fucked her.

She knew just where to touch, and her fingers flew over her skin as her orgasm overtook her. "Yes," she cried as her muscles clenched around Jake's hand. "Don't stop! Oh God, don't stop."

As Sandy prolonged her orgasm, Jake's fingers filled her. When it was over, the two lovers collapsed. It took a few minutes for her to catch her breath.

Jake sighed. "I've never felt anything like that. When you climaxed with my hand inside of you, I could feel all of it." His voice was warm and loving. "Usually when you come, I'm otherwise occupied."

"How did it feel?" Sandy asked softly, fascinated by the sound of wonder in his voice.

"I could feel all your muscles as you came. It was like you were pulling me inside of you. I actually got almost the same kind of pleasure from your climax as I do out of my own."

"It was okay, what I did?"

Jake raised himself on one elbow and looked into Sandy's eyes. "It was magnificent. I loved it. Was that very difficult for you?"

"In the beginning, I was very embarrassed. But eventually . . ."

"Yeah." Jake giggled. "I know. Me, too."

"That was wonderful."

Tangled in each other, they fell asleep.

As you have seen, showing and/or telling your partner what gives pleasure and what doesn't requires some understanding from both parties. Jake was so right when he asked whether he was supposed to guess. Too many of us think that a bit of body language or a few slight shifts of position will be sufficient to tell our partner how to move, what to touch. And when that isn't enough, we try again once or twice, then give up and settle for the usual.

Your partner is probably just as frustrated. He senses that something's not perfect, not the way he wants it to be, but he doesn't know how to fix it. He tries to discover what's needed, but maybe he isn't as brave as Jake was, brave enough to ask out loud. So he flounders, fumbles, then gives up and settles for the status quo.

Sad, isn't it? Both of you want what gives pleasure. You want the same thing! Help each other.

The problems are different, but no less important, for a newly partnered couple of greater experience. Many new relationships are formed between individuals who have been involved with others previously. Second and third marriages are more the norm than the exception—couples who are now trying to create satisfying relationships, having had permanent partners prior to this. This causes new problems.

Maybe you were happy with your previous partner and want to mold your new one into the image of that person. Sexually, you want the same type of foreplay and you want intercourse in the same sort of position and with the same timing and denouement that you had before. But your partner does, too, and there's the problem. You probably don't want exactly the same things.

The answer? Communication. There are no great lovers, only great partnerships. Talk with your partner. If you have trouble broaching the subject, have a glass of wine, a beer, or a drink, then relax and cuddle. However, don't get so tipsy that you lose control over your mouth. This is a delicate process.

Try beginning with the things you don't like, explaining them, perhaps, in the context of previous experiences.

"I had a lover once who liked to make love on the living-room carpet. I thought it would be fun, but I ended up with the worst rug burn on my bottom."

"I had one who enjoyed making love in the shower. It was really nice until he got soap in my vagina. It burned like hell and I was too embarrassed to mention it."

This kind of lighthearted discussion can lead to more serious topics. Take care, however, not to get into a "let's knock our previous partner" contest. That's a sure loser, since it puts your current partner in competition with your previous one. This is a new relationship and should chart its own course.

While you're laughing about negative experiences, listen carefully. Extend your personal antenna and try to hear the truths that might be hidden inside the jests. Carol found out some interesting things when she and her new husband, Barry, had such a conversation.

CAROL AND BARRY'S STORY

"I remember one man," Carol said, snuggled against her husband, Barry, on the sofa one Tuesday evening, "who made love to me and never took off his socks."

"You're kidding!"

"Nope. One evening, he kept his undershirt on, too. He said that when he did his next load of laundry, the semen stains would remind him of me. That was the last evening I ever spent with him."

Barry's laugh was forced. "I know you had lovers before we met, but it still makes me a bit jealous."

"Me, too. About your women, I mean. But whatever happened is in the past now." Carol cuddled closer and put her hand on her husband's chest, her head in the crook of his shoulder. "What was your worst?"

Barry smiled. "Hair spray. This girl I dated . . . well, she had hair like straw, and when I finally got her into bed, it looked like the scarecrow from *The Wizard of Oz*. It took days to get the smell of that sticky stuff out of my nose."

Carol chuckled. "Don't say anything—I used to use lots of that stuff."

Barry ruffled Carol's hair. "I'm glad you don't do that anymore."

"Your talk about smells reminds me: I dated a guy who smoked. He started to kiss me, but I couldn't do it. His breath was so nasty that I went home. Just like that." Carol hesitated. "Did you ever want to do something that a girl didn't like?"

Barry got a faraway look in his eyes. "There was a girl once. Her name was Marge. God, I loved her tits almost as much as I love yours. They were big, pillowy, soft." Barry reached over and stroked Carol's large breasts through her sweater.

"What did you want her to do that she didn't want to?"

Barry shifted position and tightened his arm around Carol's shoulder. "You'll think this is gross."

"No. I promise I won't."

Barry tweaked Carol's nipples through the fabric. "I wanted more than anything for her to let me rub my cock between her tits."

"Really?"

"Okay, maybe I'm some kind of pervert, but that's what I wanted."

Carol glanced at Barry's crotch and saw the unmistakable bulge their conversation had created. She sat up, pulled off her sweater and bra, and knelt on the floor between Barry's feet. She quickly unzipped his fly and took out his hard cock. "How?" She leaned forward and captured his member between her large breasts. "Like this?" She pressed the palms of her hands against the sides of her breasts and moved up and down, fucking his cock with her tits.

"Shit, honey," Barry groaned. "Just like that. But it needs to be slippery." He dipped his fingers into the water glass on the coffee table and rubbed the cold liquid in the valley between Carol's breasts. Then he held his cock as she grasped it between her now-wet globes. It took only moments before he was spurting come all over his jeans and shirt, covering Carol's chest, as well.

Later, he said, "That's been a fantasy of mine for so long that I couldn't wait. I'm sorry it was so fast."

"And you should be sorry," Carol teased. "But maybe I can figure out a way for you to make it up to me."

"Oh?" Barry said, one eyebrow raised.

"Actually, I have a few things I've always wanted."

"Name them," Barry said, grinning. "I dare you."

If you are newly partnered and have had previous long-term partners, you and your ex had certain understandings, whether you realize it or not. Maybe you never made love on Fridays. Or perhaps you made love only after eleven in the evening. Or, like me, you may never have made love while you had your period. See whether you can discover what those rules were, although they usually evolve so subtly that you're not aware you even had rules. When you discover one of those "Goes without saying" regulations, decide whether it's one to keep—like my aversion to making love while menstruating—or one that should be reconsidered—like never making love outside the bedroom.

I've had three long-term relationships in my life: my marriage, a six-year partnership, and my current twelve-year partnership with Ed. In each relationship, my partner and I had to establish new ground rules and discover all over again the things that gave each of us joy. And, surprisingly enough, those things changed. You may have given up the idea of some activity because your previous partner didn't enjoy it. Now you have the opportunity to try all over again. Hooray for new relationships.

One part of establishing a monogamous relationship is birth control. You've probably already begun to discuss family planning, but if you need more specific information, consult your doctor or do some simple research. Having children is the most important decision you and your partner may ever make. If she becomes pregnant, let it be because you both wanted it, not because of ignorance.

There are many things that do *not* prevent pregnancy—for example, douching, making love standing up, and withdrawing before ejaculation. If you want details about why these don't work, check with your doctor or a text on the subject. But trust me. They don't.

Also, there are those who believe that if a woman doesn't have an orgasm, she can't conceive; that a woman can't conceive while she has her period or while she's nursing; or that she can't conceive during her very first sexual experience. Unfortunately, all those myths are just that—myths.

Men and women used to soak in hot baths to "kill all the sperm and eggs" right before intercourse. That didn't work, either.

Many women believe that douching with any number of concoctions—from vinegar to soapy water to over-the-counter products—right before or after copulation will also prevent conception. Wrong.

A warning: Let's take a moment to discuss douching. Don't douche. Many doctors believe that commercially available douches and/or douching with vinegar or other liquids can upset the bacterial balance of your vagina and lead to irritation and infection. So don't be sold on the "feeling fresh" advertising. A woman who bathes and/or showers regularly will be fresh. If you really don't feel clean or odorless and it's interfering with your sex life, shower right before sex—together.

As far as selecting the proper method of birth control, check with your doctor and discuss it at length with your partner. There are many options available and more on the way, since the FDA perpetually has products in the approval process. Each method has its advantages and disadvantages, so for each couple it is a personal choice. But whatever you use, use it regularly. Don't miss that pill. Use that foam or sponge precisely according to the manufacturer's directions. Be sure that your diaphragm is filled with plenty of spermicidal gel and in place every night, whether you plan to have sex or not. That allows for spontaneity, with no unexpected surprises nine months later.

A few words about condoms. First, although natural skins do prevent unwanted pregnancy as well as any other condom, they do not protect either partner from sexually transmitted diseases. If you and your partner have been monogamous for more than five years, this might be all right, but why take the chance? Latex condoms really are new and improved, and they now come in colors, flavors, and textures, lubricated and nonlubricated. There was a story on the radio recently about a Hungarian company that developed a musical condom that plays a tune as it is unrolled. (I wonder what song it plays.)

You can even buy assortment packages by mail from many catalog companies so you can try and compare. Ed and I have tried several types, with ribs, ticklers, nubs. I must tell you that I didn't notice any difference, but you might. So experiment with lots of different ones. In the back of my book *Come Play with Me*, there is a list of some of the many companies that will send catalogs to you.

Latex condoms fit pretty much everyone, but if the man's cock is particularly small or particularly large, be sure you buy a condom that fits properly and doesn't come off during intercourse or restrict blood flow.

It is important to put a condom on properly. It must be put on before *any* penis-vagina contact. Playing with a loaded weapon is not permitted. A man's lubricating fluid—or "pre-come," as it is often called—is full of sperm, and those little devils can travel upstream from even the most casual vaginal contact. Put the condom on properly and carefully before any intimate genital contact.

By the way, it can be fun to let your partner help put it on—*very slowly.*

After ejaculation, it is important to remove the condom-covered penis from the vagina before the penis softens, so there is no leakage of fluid around the penis. Hold the base of the condom while withdrawing carefully. Then, once the condom-covered penis is out of contact with the vagina, remove the condom carefully and don't make contact with any vaginal tissues. Sperm are resourceful and have only one purpose—the one you're trying to prevent. And never reuse a condom—ever.

Okay, now you're together permanently, every night. What does that mean? For one, it means that being together isn't a date anymore. A lot of people ask each other, "What are we going to do tonight?" You see each other naked every night, so it's not an exciting novelty anymore. Sex tends to begin in the same way, progress along familiar paths, and end up in the same place, the bedroom. Now it's predictable. And what's wrong with that? I hear you ask. Nothing. But predictability can lead to boredom, and that is a problem.

This is a time to be a bit creative, but creativity requires communication. You and your partner must find a way to share your needs, desires, and fantasies. There are several important parts to good communication, some of which we've already read about with Jake and Sandy and with Barry and Carol.

First is the willingness to take a bit of risk. Let's say

that, like Barry, you've had a fantasy for years. You have recurrent dreams about having your partner show up at your office at lunchtime, lock the office door, and ravish you in your desk chair. Wonderful. But discussing that with your partner is a delicate matter.

He'll think I'm crazy.

She'll think I'm kinky.

He'll think he's not good enough for me.

She'll think our sex life isn't any good.

He'll think I'm not a good lover.

She'll think I'm not a good lover.

Personally, I think the risk is minimal with two people who genuinely want to please each other. Suggest something mild at first. Use body language, purrs and groans, subtle ways to say "I like that," or "That doesn't feel as nice as what you were doing before." While making love, tell a story that includes something you want to try. Slip a bookmark in one of the stories in this book. However you do it, take a chance.

The second requirement for good communication is being a good receiver. Tune your radar to your partner's frequency if that person is telling you a story or a joke. Look for suggestions everywhere—in conversation, in gestures, in responsiveness. Resist knee-jerk reactions. Just relax and realize that your partner's telling you something wonderful, sharing difficult yet potentially highly exciting things with you. He or she has made the first move toward better communication. It's up to you to make the second. Discuss or slowly act on what you think you've discovered. Rub that way instead of this, and listen.

But what if you hate the idea your partner suggests? It is as important to say no as it is to say yes.

Lovemaking must never become an endurance contest, testing yourself to see whether you can put up with that awful thing your partner wants to try. If you've got an open mind about rubbing grape jelly on each other's bellies, go for it. But if the entire idea makes you gag, say so. Neither of you want a negative encounter, because it makes the next one that much more difficult. So say, "I don't think I would enjoy that." Then add, "But I might like it if we . . ."

Saying no has a positive side, too. Ed and I communicate well, and occasionally one or the other of us has suggested something that the other finds unpleasant. If I know that he will admit that an idea of mine turns him off, I can suggest anything—literally. So can he. I don't have to worry that he's enduring something for my sake, and I don't endure for his. Whatever we do is for the right reasons.

Since Al and Tina each had good radar, they learned something new about each other one afternoon, totally by accident.

AL AND TINA'S STORY

Al worked for a large suburban manufacturing firm, and the low industrial buildings covered a large area. The company had landscaped the acres around the buildings carefully, with large wooded areas and artificially created ponds and streams. Animal life was abundant in secluded glens and clearings that contained bird and small-animal feeders. In the nice weather, both at lunchtime and after work, these areas were filled with employees. They wandered through the lush foliage or sat on blankets to watch the birds and to hand-feed the tame squirrels.

Tina had the day off from work. Since it was late May and a perfect day for a picnic, she surprised her husband with a wicker basket in one hand and a thick plaid blanket under her other arm. It took no time for Al to put his work aside, find a spot, spread the blanket, and devour the sumptuous lunch Tina had assembled. "It's so beautiful out here," Tina said. Content, she dropped onto her back and gazed at the fragments of brilliant blue sky visible through the leaves of the huge maple tree above them.

"And you're a sexy broad," Al said, watching the way her position caused her lightweight summer blouse to stretch across her ample bosom.

"Umm," she purred. "And you're a very sexy man." She let her eyes roam her husband's body and her gaze settled on the lump in the front of his pants. She watched him shift position as he sat on the blanket.

"You make me crazy," he said, then he looked at his watch. "Damn, it's almost one-thirty. I was due back fifteen minutes ago."

He started to get up, but Tina took his hand. "You're late already. Will anyone really miss you for another few minutes? It's so wonderful here."

Al settled back down. "Well," he mused aloud, "Mark's away today and Georgia had a dentist appointment."

"So you can stay a few more minutes?"

"I guess." He settled back onto the blanket, lying shoulder-to-shoulder with Tina, their fingers intertwined. "This makes me think of our honeymoon.

Remember? We got so excited that we almost tore each other's clothes off on the beach that day."

"God I was hot," Tina said, feeling her excitement grow as she remembered. "We almost ran to the room."

"I always wondered how it would have felt to do it right there on the beach."

"Al," Tina said, shocked, "you wouldn't have. There were people around."

"I know, but making love in the open just seems so erotic."

"Someone might have seen us."

"So? We're married. And we're only doing what everyone knows people do every day." He turned and tickled the inside of Tina's ear with the tip of his tongue.

"Al, stop that." She playfully pushed him away. "There are people here, too."

Al propped himself up on one elbow. "Not really. Lunch hour's long over. There's no one in sight." He squeezed her breast.

Despite her better judgment, Tina was getting very excited by the conversation and by Al's talented hand. Her husband was usually very traditional about love-making, preferring the bedroom at night. This was so thrillingly risky. "You wouldn't dare." She didn't know whether she wanted him to dare or not.

Al looked at Tina's slightly flushed face and saw the rapid rise and fall of her chest. The idea obviously excited her as much as it did him. "No one would know." He ran his finger over the crotch of Tina's jeans and felt her heat. He watched her breathing quicken even more and felt her hips move. "You know," he whispered, "it's more exciting knowing that there might be people watching us."

Tina was silent. It *was* exciting thinking of someone possibly seeing what they were doing. And Al's hand rubbing her crotch was driving her crazy. After a while, she murmured, "You'd better stop that."

"Why?" Al asked, his face close to her ear, so his hot breath tickled her.

"Because."

"Because you're going to come? Tell me." His finger rubbed all the places he knew she liked, and he could feel the crotch of her jeans getting damp.

"Oh God, baby."

"I know we can't fuck right now, but I'm going to make you come. Right here, where anyone might be watching." His finger kept up its magic rhythm. "Maybe someone's got a pair of binoculars and is peering at us through the trees. Maybe he can see my hand between your legs."

"Baby . . ." The thought of someone watching her filled Tina's mind with erotic images: A strange man's eyes, his knowing that Tina was going to come.

"Maybe it makes him hot to watch what we're doing. Maybe he'll take out his dick and start playing with it while he watches us. He's got his dick in one hand and his binoculars in the other. He's watching us and jerking off."

The image of the man with his engorged penis in his hand was enough to drive Tina over the edge. With little noise or movement, the first spasm hit her.

"Oh yes, baby," Al purred. "Come for me while that man watches."

Waves of orgasm rolled over Tina's body, flowing

from her belly to her sopping cunt. Her mind swirled with Al's hand, the unseen man's cock, the binoculars.

"He's watching us," Al whispered, "seeing my hand rub your pussy. His eyes are on my hand and on your face. He knows you're coming. You can't hide from his eyes."

Al's voice drove spasm after spasm through her body. "Oh God, baby," she moaned again. "Oh God. So good."

Finally limp, Tina lay beside Al in silence for a while, then said, "That was sensational. I'd never imagined that the idea of someone watching me would get me so turned on."

"Neither did I. But you just went crazy. God you were hot."

"But what about you?" She patted his crotch. "You didn't come."

"I know. But I want to wait until later. I'm not quite the exhibitionist that you are."

"Exhibitionist?" Tina said, horrified. "I am not."

"Well, maybe it's just the fantasy of being watched, but it sure got to you. And I can wait. Now that I know what makes you go crazy, I want to consider all the other places we can make love. The top of the Empire State Building, the White House lawn . . ."

TRY SOMETHING NEW: VIDEOS

If you enjoy the fantasy of being watched, the video camera might be just the thing for you.

It is said that X-rated videos appeal mostly to men.

Ed and I seem to have been born the wrong sexes. Most X-rated videos turn him off, but they turn me on. So much for common wisdom. Suffice it to say that if X-rated videos turn you on, rent one or two and watch them together.

Buying videos is an expensive proposition. I get lots of catalogs with hundreds of videos described, at prices ranging from ten dollars for amateur films made by couples not unlike you and your partner to seventy and eighty dollars for movies specializing in bondage, spanking, and other such activities. Unfortunately, if you're interested in such specialties, they aren't always easy to rent, so purchasing might be your only alternative.

You can play a game with an X-rated video. Set a timer for anywhere from five minutes after the movie begins to a few minutes before its conclusion. Then, when the timer sounds, do whatever the folks in the film are doing. Silly but fun, and fun's what it's all about, after all.

You can also make your own video. The nice thing about video cameras is that you don't have to have your film developed, so you can film whatever you like without the danger of anyone else seeing what you were doing. Set the camera on a solid surface or on a tripod, aim it at the bed, press the record button, and cavort. It can be just as exhilarating to watch the film later.

If you've got a friend with whom you are particularly close, you can have him or her film your lovemaking. Particularly thrilling can be having that person direct the lovemaking, giving you instructions as to how and where to touch and what to do.

TRY SOMETHING NEW:
COMPUTERS AND CYBERSEX

Computers used to be limited to office use, but since the proliferation of smaller, more affordable models, many households now have a home computer. Because of the privacy this affords, many companies have jumped into the X-rated market. There is an amazing variety of X-rated games and CD-ROM movies. I recently played a version of the spacial-relations game Tetris in which every time you scored points, a woman at one side of the screen removed some of her clothes. Eventually, she was nude, and then another picture appeared. For those who enjoy watching women strip photographically, it added extra incentive to the game.

Then, of course, there's cyberspace. The World Wide Web. The Internet. You can't exist for more than twenty-four hours right now without hearing about, reading about, learning about, or being mystified about this magical place. Everyone has a Web site, from *Time* magazine to your local car dealer. Your next-door neighbor has one that displays pictures of his kids. Your favorite TV channel has one with coming attractions and advertisements.

Whether you think that the World Wide Web is the greatest invention since sliced bread or the largest assortment of computerized junk mail ever assembled, it's here and it's real and it's got some interesting material for the sexually curious.

The Internet is a busy place. I've only touched the surface in my personal explorations. Here's what I found.

There are numerous collections of erotic stories for downloading and reading. Some are good stories from both new and experienced writers interested in displaying and receiving responses to soft-core and hardcore material of all types. Needless to say, some are awful, but some are clever and well written. Some are depictions of ordinary lovemaking; some are more off-center; and some are truly bizarre. Some will appeal to you; some may not. Browse, read what you enjoy, and use your delete key for the rest.

There are sexually oriented World Wide Web sites to appeal to every taste, from those interested in meeting members of the opposite or the same sex to professional "entertainers" with 900 phone numbers. There are sites put up by people of every sexual persuasion in search of people with like interests to correspond or chat with, from lesbians to transvestites. A few hours of Net surfing will turn up a variety of cyberlocations.

Pictures are available on the Internet. You can browse the Louvre. You can look at people during various stages of any type of sexual encounter you can imagine. As before, download what appeals to you and pass on the rest.

A warning: You will probably stumble onto pictures of minors engaged in sexual activities. Don't download those. They are illegal and can get you into all forms of legal difficulties. If you are offered pictures from someone you meet on-line, again beware.

Computer on-line services are everywhere, from Prodigy, CompuServe, and America Online to small local Internet-access providers. And with these services come the chat rooms, and in some of the chat rooms you can find amazingly new sexual experiences.

What's sex on-line like? Well, it's like phone sex in writing, but usually both parties are giving and receiving. To my mind, "hot chatting," as it's called, is a lot less threatening than listening to a live voice. Why would you want to try it? Well, here's how I began.

I am a longtime user of one of the large on-line service companies and I had been talking with other members in an area devoted to writers, helping answer questions about plot, characterization, editors, agents, and the like.

One evening, I decided to try one of the general chat rooms. I entered a room full of over thirties and lurked for a bit, just watching the questions, answers, and comments scroll across my screen. It took me awhile to become accustomed to several conversations taking place at the same time, but when I learned to read every third, fourth, or fifth line and to keep track of who was discussing what with whom, I was able to follow the interaction easily.

Once or twice, something caught my eye and I typed an answer to a question or a comment someone else had written. It was interesting, but only mildly. I knew, of course, about the more esoteric rooms and, with a few clicks of my mouse, I found myself in Truth or Dare.

Wow. There were supposedly more than twenty people in that room but only four or five were chatting. (Please note that none of the conversations here are real, nor are the screen names. And I've simplified things to only one conversation at a time.)

ANDY: Truth or dare?
JENNY: Truth
ANDY: Tell me about the most unusual place you ever made love

• • •

Jenny proceeded to tell Andy about making love in a cemetery—in lurid detail. I was fascinated and titillated. Suddenly, someone typed

DON: Hey Joan, age/sex, please

I decided that I could take a few liberties with the truth.

JOAN: I'm female and 35. You?

I haven't been thirty-five in almost twenty years, but in cyberspace, you can be whoever and whatever you like. It's all really harmless.

DON: 24/male. T/d?

Maybe he was and maybe not; I didn't really care. But I realized that he was asking me whether I wanted a truth or a dare.

JOAN: Truth
DON: What are you wearing?

Again I could make up an answer, and I did.

Well, you get the idea. I spent an incredible two hours talking dirty to people, changing rooms, cyber-experiencing everything from medieval dungeons to the hot tub, from "Women for women" to "Ask a man anything." I had a blast, and the following evening, when I told Ed about my experience, I had another wonderful time.

A warning: One of the advantages to being on-line is also one of the biggest problems. Not only are you anonymous but so is everyone else. You have no idea what kind of person you're talking to. So be sensible.

A further warning: Never use your full real name or give out any accurate personal information, especially your address or phone number. I've been asked many times for my phone number so someone I've spent an enjoyable time with could call and continue "more personally." This is not for me. I told one cyberpartner that I wouldn't give out my phone number, so he suggested that I call him. I wouldn't do that, either. Caller ID can give someone your phone number without your knowing it. The phone company tells me that by dialing a particular code, you can disable caller ID so the person you call cannot get your number. Maybe you can, but I'm just not that trusting.

There are happy exceptions, of course. Many people, including a couple I know, have met and fallen in love on-line. If you eventually learn to trust the person with whom you're chatting, let your good sense be your guide.

In addition, try to establish that your chat partner is over eighteen. I always ask, but, as we know, many people lie. Sometimes you can tell the age of a counterpart by the nature of the questions. Personally, I automatically reject anyone who asks my bra size. It's a juvenile question and shows an attitude, if not a chronological age, that is younger than that of someone I want to play with. You may find your own limits. I'm not going to go into the issue of limiting a minor's access to sexually explicit material here. I'm just suggesting caution.

I had one experience during which, for some reason, the guy I was playing with suddenly asked, "Are you really a woman?"

"Yes," I answered.

"How can I be sure?" he typed, paranoia dripping from each word.

"I don't know," I replied. Obviously, I couldn't find any way to reassure him, and I found that his fears were ruining my enjoyment. I signed off soon thereafter. The fact that I may have had cybersex with women doesn't faze me. It was all in good fun.

If you want to play in depth, go to a private room. On AOL and probably many other services, it is possible to create a private room, a place where only you and other invited guests can chat. The general chat rooms are open and anyone can bop in at any time. You can be observed by minors at any time, even accidentally, and you don't want that to happen.

A suggestion: Anytime you begin to feel uncomfortable about what's going on, sign off.

MARY KATE'S STORY

Mary Kate had been married for several years and had recently gotten a computer to help organize the family finances. The machine came with access to an online service and, using her free hours, she had begun to explore the service's chat rooms.

One evening, while her husband, Greg, was at a business meeting, Mary Kate logged on as 1ShyGirl and ventured into a room named Beginners to CyberSex. She got to chatting with a man who had logged on as 4NewGames. When he suggested that they continue in a private room, she agreed.

4NEWGAMES: Welcome to our private room.

1SHYGIRL: This is the first time I've been in a private room with anyone

4NEWGAMES: I'm glad I'm your first. That's why I spend time in that particular cyberchat room. In a room called Beginners to Cybersex I run into lots of new people like you. I enjoy that a lot. Now we're together where we can talk, just the two of us. Just tell me the truth and I'll teach you all about on-line sexual fun.

1SHYGIRL: Okay. I'm really nervous. I don't know what to do.

4NEWGAMES: That's okay. I do. What's your first name?

1SHYGIRL: Mary

4NEWGAMES: That's very plain. I like to think of you as extraordinary. Do you have a middle name?

1SHYGIRL: Katherine

4NEWGAMES: Good, Mary Katherine. No, too long to type. Mary Kate. That's good. New things for us to do--a new name for you. I like that. And my name's Peter. What are you wearing right now, Mary Kate?

1SHYGIRL: I'm wearing a T-shirt and shorts.

4NEWGAMES: Undies?

1SHYGIRL: Yes. Bra and panties.

4NEWGAMES: Will you do something for me, and then we'll talk a bit?

1SHYGIRL: What?

4NEWGAMES: I'd like you to take off your bra, then put your shirt back on. Just that. Will you do that for me, Mary Kate?

1SHYGIRL: I guess

4NEWGAMES:	I would like that, but if you don't want to, just tell me. I want to picture you as you actually are. Will you take your bra off? For me? No one but you and I will know.
1SHYGIRL:	Yes--I'm doing that now
4NEWGAMES:	While you're doing that, just read the screen. I'm 35 years old, divorced, and I have fantasies about making love to women who've never had a creative lover before. When you have your shirt back on, type "here."
1SHYGIRL:	Here
4NEWGAMES:	Good. Tell me, does it feel sort of slutty to have your nipples rubbing against the inside of your T-shirt?
1SHYGIRL:	Yes
4NEWGAMES:	Nice?
1SHYGIRL:	Yes
4NEWGAMES:	I knew you'd like the feeling. From what you said in the main room, I know you're 32. Are you married?
1SHYGIRL:	I got married about a year ago.
4NEWGAMES:	Do you and your husband have a good sex life?
1SHYGIRL:	You ask embarrassing questions
4NEWGAMES:	I do, and you don't have to answer. But I'd like to know so we can have the most fun together tonight. We're anonymous. I'll never meet you for real and you'll never meet me. You can tell me anything and no one will ever know.
1SHYGIRL:	Greg would like me to be a little more creative, but . . . Well . . . I just don't know much.

4NEWGAMES: Okay. Not too much experience. That's fine. Just the kind of girl I hoped you'd be. Where is Greg tonight?

1SHYGIRL: He's got a business meeting. He'll be home later.

4NEWGAMES: Maybe if we have some fun tonight, you and he can play together when he gets home.

1SHYGIRL: Maybe. I'd sure like to make him happy. And this is really making me excited.

4NEWGAMES: Don't be too surprised at anything you feel tonight. Many of the things we'll do together will surprise you, but it will be a nice surprise.

1SHYGIRL: I know. I'm surprised at myself already

4NEWGAMES: Tell me--are you really excited being here with me?

1SHYGIRL: Yes, I am

4NEWGAMES: That's soooo good. May I touch your face?

1SHYGIRL: I guess

4NEWGAMES: I'm touching your cheeks. They are very soft. I'm touching your eyebrows and your temples. Very soft caresses, just brushing over your skin. I'm tangling my fingers in your hair. It's soft and I love to feel it between my fingers. What color is it? No, wait. What color would you like it to be? Create a new you for me.

1SHYGIRL: My hair is blond, long, and wavy.

4NEWGAMES: Good. I love to run my fingers through it. It's so long and soft. Like spun gold. I pull a long strand forward and let it fall down the front of your shirt. It curls

	around your breast. Can you feel your hair tickling your nipple as it lies against your shirt?
1SHYGIRL:	Yes, I can
4NEWGAMES:	Rub your open palm over your hard nipple. Feel how erect it is, like a hard little nub in your hand. You're hesitating. I know it. Don't. It's your body and you have permission to touch it whenever you want to. Make it feel good. You know you want to, and you're all alone. Just you and me, and I can only imagine. Please touch it. Feel how good it is. Pretend that it's my hand, but just do it. Tell me you touched your aroused body.
1SHYGIRL:	Yes. I did
4NEWGAMES:	Wonderful. That was difficult for you but rewarding. Wasn't it? No lightning struck you, did it?
1SHYGIRL:	No
4NEWGAMES:	No voices cried that you were BAD. It just felt good, didn't it? Tell me, Mary Kate. Admit to me and to yourself that it felt good. Just say yes.
1SHYGIRL:	Yes
4NEWGAMES:	Would you take off your shirt for me, Mary Kate? I want to be able to picture your beautiful breasts. Will you do that for me?
1SHYGIRL:	Yes. You know, I'm really surprised by what I'm doing tonight. I really am going to take off my shirt.
4NEWGAMES:	Oh baby. You're so good. I'm picturing you pulling your shirt over your head.

Your long blond hair curls down your chest and around your breasts. Run your fingers through it while I do that, too.

1SHYGIRL: Yes

4NEWGAMES: Your hair feels so wonderful. I'm letting it fall against your nipples. I can see they are hard and tight.

1SHYGIRL: Yes

4NEWGAMES: I'm running my fingers through your hair, and brushing my fingertips against your nipple at the same time. The right one.

1SHYGIRL: I'm embarrassed now

4NEWGAMES: That's okay. That heightens the feelings. Just go with it. There's nothing wrong with anything we're doing. I'm just touching one bare breast. I want to kiss you. I'm holding your breast while I lean close. You have a beautiful soft mouth just made for kissing.

1SHYGIRL: I do?

4NEWGAMES: You know you do, Mary Kate. You know you taste good. But we both need more now, don't we? Say yes if you want more. Tell me, baby.

1SHYGIRL: Yes

4NEWGAMES: Take off your shorts and panties while I picture how you look. Do it just for me, Mary Kate. No one else will know. You're getting me all excited, Mary Kate. I'm getting very hard just thinking about you. Are you undressed now?

1SHYGIRL: Yes. I really am.

4NEWGAMES: Oh God, you're perfect. I want to kiss

	your nipple, but I want you to let me do it. Tell me yes.
1SHYGIRL:	Yes
4NEWGAMES:	Oh baby. I'm touching my lips to your right nipple. It's hard and pointed, reaching for me. I'm sucking the tip into my mouth. My mouth is so hot, so wet. I've wet your nipple. Now I'll blow on it.
1SHYGIRL:	That's cold
4NEWGAMES:	Yes, it is. But it feels wonderful and makes you hot.
1SHYGIRL:	Yes
4NEWGAMES:	While I suck one nipple, I squeeze the other between my thumb and index finger. Do you like it when I squeeze it? Can you feel it?
1SHYGIRL:	yesss
4NEWGAMES:	Do it with me. Touch your nipples like I am. Feel it so good. While I'm touching you, I'm touching myself, too.
1SHYGIRL:	Really? Are you excted? I mean, excited?
4NEWGAMES:	I'm chuckling. I like the typos. They tell me you're too excited to type well. And yes, I'm reallllly excited. But I can still type, too. Are you touching your beautiful breasts?
1SHYGIRL:	Yes
4NEWGAMES:	I want to touch more of you. You have your knees together. Part your legs for me. Do it, baby
1SHYGIRL:	Yes
4NEWGAMES:	I have my palm flat on your belly, my fingers just brushing your pussy hair. I'm sorry. Does the word "pussy" offend you?

1SHYGIRL: No, I guess not. It belongs here. In private. Just between us.

4NEWGAMES: Yes, it does. Now I'm very slowly moving my fingers lower. Tell me, Mary Kate, are you wet?

1SHYGIRL: Oh yes, very

4NEWGAMES: I want you to feel where you're wet. Have you ever touched your body like that? Rubbed where it feels good?

1SHYGIRL: No. It's bad.

4NEWGAMES: No, it's not bad. It feels good. Bodies were made to feel good so people would do the silly things we do during sex. Will you do just one thing for me? If you do, you'll like it. But if by some chance you don't, just tell me. Okay?

1SHYGIRL: okay

4NEWGAMES: I want you to take one finger and touch where it's wet. Just touch it gently. Will you do that for me? For us? Please?

1SHYGIRL: difficult

4NEWGAMES: I know. But you're all alone. No one can see you. And you know how good it will feel. Please. Just touch. While you decide, let me tell you what I'm doing. My cock is very hard. It's so hard, it actually hurts. I haven't been so turned on in a long time. Just thinking about how good you will feel later makes me sooo hungry. Part of me wants to be there with you, to share in person. But part of me knows that if I was there, you wouldn't feel as free as you do now. Do you feel free with me?

1SHYGIRL:	Yes
4NEWGAMES:	Will you touch yourself for me?
1SHYGIRL:	All right
4NEWGAMES:	I know it's difficult to type now. And it's even more difficult to talk/type about what you feel, but please--tell me--how does it feel to touch yourself?
1SHYGIRL:	good-- strange-- so exciting-- feels good--
4NEWGAMES:	You're typing slowly. I like that. Will you keep rubbing where it feels good?
1SHYGIRL:	Yes--
4NEWGAMES:	Oh baby, you make me so hot--if I rub my cock, I'll come right here, right now
1SHYGIRL:	Do that
4NEWGAMES:	Oh Mary Kate--hard to type now. I want to give you more, but I need it so much. Coming--hard to breathe
1SHYGIRL:	are you? Coming, I mean? Really?
4NEWGAMES:	yesssssssss--shit minute. Phew Panting Wow Phew Better . . . Now for you. Rub where it feels good. Rub. Find your own rhythm. Feel it in your belly. Reach for it low in your belly. Rub. Do whatever feels good. Please, baby. I want it for you and I can't do it for you. I wish I could. Picture my fingers between your legs, rubbing, stroking, caressing your lips,

your clit. I know just where to touch--
your fingers know, too. Touch it now.

1SHYGIRL: yes
              yes
              yes

4NEWGAMES: tell me baby

1SHYGIRL: oh god
              yes

4NEWGAMES: did it happen for you?

1SHYGIRL: will

4NEWGAMES: Picture my mouth on your breast, suck-
              ing while my fingers invade your pussy.
              I'm sucking, stroking, and sliding one
              finger inside of you. Making love to you
              in every way I can

1SHYGIRL: god yes

4NEWGAMES: I'm adding another finger, filling your
              pussy, stretching it. Feeling the slick walls
              of your channel. I can feel your climax
              coming--reach for it--pull it closer--tell
              me--come for me, Mary Kate

1SHYGIRL: god yes
              now

4NEWGAMES: Make it feel good--do whatever it takes
              for you to feel good.

1SHYGIRL: came--
              panting--
              never like that before

4NEWGAMES: You make me so happy. I love giving
              pleasure--and getting it, too. There's so
              much for us to explore. We can play any
              game we want. Be anything, anyone we
              want. You can explore your own sensu-
              ality with me or by yourself. You can

visit the member rooms like Le Château, where they get into bondage games, or The Hot Tub, where they have cyberorgies every night, or play Truth or Dare in cyberspace. If you tire of one vision of yourself, change your screen name and become someone else. Be the virginal schoolgirl, the dominant female, the harem dancer--whatever you like.

1SHYGIRL:	I think I could
4NEWGAMES:	I have to go now and get cleaned up. Will you dream of me and all the pleasures there are for us? For you?
1SHYGIRL:	Count on it
4NEWGAMES:	Will you meet me again?
1SHYGIRL:	Count on that, too
4NEWGAMES:	Think about bringing your husband next time. We can play together.
1SHYGIRL:	Maybe I will. That would sure surprise him.
4NEWGAMES:	I'm sure it would. Good night, Mary Kate
1SHYGIRL:	Good night

MARY KATE AND GREG'S STORY

When Greg got home later that evening, Mary Kate, dressed in a filmy nightgown and peignoir set she hadn't worn since their honeymoon, greeted him at the door. Before he was through the door, she pressed her body against his and kissed him, driving her tongue deep into his mouth. Greg dropped his briefcase and held her tightly. "Not that I'm complaining," he said when they finally parted, "but what was that for?"

"I'll tell you all about it later," Mary said, pulling Greg's arms from the sleeves of his jacket. She was surprised at how brave and aggressive she felt. She realized that she didn't want to make love to Greg—she wanted to fuck his brains out. She almost dragged him into the bedroom, and as soon as they were both naked, she grasped his already-hard cock and pulled him on top of her. Their lovemaking was hard and quick and thoroughly satisfying for them both.

When they had calmed, Mary slowly told Greg about her encounter with 4NewGames. Greg listened in silence, trying not to let his mouth hang open. When she had finished, he said, "You really did that?"

Suddenly shy again, Mary remained silent. She knew that Greg could feel her withdrawing, and then she felt his arms holding her close. "I think that's fantastic," he said. "I've tried every way I could think of to help you realize how much more there is to lovemaking, but it seems that you found a way to learn all by yourself."

"You really don't mind?"

"Mind?" Greg said, hugging her still more tightly. "I think it's great."

Mary hesitated. "While NewGames and I were . . . well, you know, I couldn't decide whether I was cheating on you."

"I don't think it's cheating if you tell me about it. If you did it in secret with no intention of ever telling me, that might be different."

Mary turned within Greg's embrace. "That's kind of the way I felt, too."

"You must have found it very exciting, judging from my reception earlier."

"Oh, I certainly did. And NewGames asked me whether I could bring you along sometime."

"You mean I could watch you while you and he play?"

Mary raised an eyebrow. "It's as close to a threesome as you'll ever get."

Greg had always fantasized about watching Mary make love to someone else, but he also realized that he wouldn't be able to deal with the jealousy. This seemed like some sort of delicious compromise. And Mary had suggested it. "That might be a gas."

It was a surprise to both Greg and Mary that their sex life changed markedly after that evening. Mary seemed more open to suggestions. They played games and ordered a few toys from a catalog. A few weeks later, Greg lay on the bed, holding Mary's hand. "Would you really consider chatting on-line while I watch?"

"Sure. But I'd tell the other person that you were there."

"That's okay, I guess."

"You never know who's on the other end of the conversation really, but not telling would feel like lying somehow."

"Yeah, I understand. Maybe you could get that guy you were with the last time."

"I could see whether he's on-line." Already excited at the possibilities this opened up, Mary got her laptop, connected the modem to the bedside phone line, and logged on. She used the "Find Another User" function and discovered that 4NewGames was logged. She sent him a message and asked if he would meet her in a private room. In a few minutes, 1ShyGirl and 4NewGames were alone together in a cyberroom called NewThings.

4NEWGAMES:	Hi, Mary Kate. How have you been? I missed you.
1SHYGIRL:	Hi. My husband's here with me.
4NEWGAMES:	Hi, husband. What's your name?
1SHYGIRL:	His name's Greg.
4NEWGAMES:	Hi, Greg. Mary Kate told you about the games we played?
1SHYGIRL:	I told him.
4NEWGAMES:	Does he want to play, too?

"Greg," Mary said, "do you want to play?"

"This is really weird, but yes, I do."

1SHYGIRL:	Yes. He says he does.
4NEWGAMES:	Great. What are you wearing, Mary Kate? And what's Greg got on?
1SHYGIRL:	I'm wearing jeans, a sweatshirt, and underwear. Greg's the same.
4NEWGAMES:	Okay. Both of you strip to the waist.

"Is this really okay?" Mary asked. "I'm really turned on."

"Me, too," Greg said as he dragged his sweatshirt off over his head.

1SHYGIRL:	Both of us are stripped. This is really strange.
4NEWGAMES:	I know, and it's really hot, isn't it?
1SHYGIRL:	Yes.

4NEWGAMES: Mary Kate, together we learned about your body. Remember? Did you tell Greg all about that?

1SHYGIRL: Yes, I remember--and yes, I did tell Greg.

4NEWGAMES: I enjoy teaching people like you about the joys of exploration. There's so much good sex.

1SHYGIRL: Like what?

4NEWGAMES: Greg, how does Mary Kate taste?

"How do you taste?" Greg said. "I never thought about that, I guess. You taste like you."

1SHYGIRL: Greg says I taste like me.

4NEWGAMES: Greg, lick Mary Kate's lips with the tip of your tongue; then take the keyboard and tell me how she tastes.

Greg licked Mary's lips, then pushed his tongue into her mouth. He explored her teeth and tongue, tasting. Then he took the laptop from Mary Kate.

1SHYGIRL: She tastes sweet, and slightly of mint. She had a Tic Tac earlier and I can still taste it.

4NEWGAMES: Good. How do her nipples taste?

Greg set the laptop aside, leaned over, and tasted Mary Kate's nipples with the flat of his tongue.

1SHYGIRL: She tastes slightly perfumy and delicious. Her nipples are getting hard now, too.

4NEWGAMES: That's good, Greg. Look at the rest of her. Can you tell that she's excited just from looking at her?

1SHYGIRL: I'm looking carefully. She's smiling, maybe a bit embarrassed by me staring at her. Her face looks soft; her lips are parted. She's flushed and she can't seem to sit still.

4NEWGAMES: How does she sound? Is she panting? Can you hear her breathing hard?

1SHYGIRL: Yes.

4NEWGAMES: Mary Kate, take off your pants and everything else you're wearing. We need to explore further.

Mary Kate stood up, pulled off her socks, jeans, and panties, and lay back down on the bed. Greg was beside her, cross-legged, with the laptop between his knees. He turned the screen so Mary Kate could again see what he was typing.

1SHYGIRL: She's naked now.

4NEWGAMES: How does she smell? Hot? Is she very aroused? Don't use anything but your sense of smell.

1SHYGIRL: Yes, she's very hot. I love the smell of her heat.

"I always hate the way I smell," Mary Kate said. "It's fishy and yucky."

"I have always loved your scent. It makes me hungry for you."

"It does?"

4NEWGAMES: Are you still there?

1SHYGIRL: Sorry. We're still here. Mary Kate doesn't think she smells good.

4NEWGAMES: I think women smell so sexy when they're hot. Don't you agree, Greg?

1SHYGIRL: I sure do. Mary Kate's looking very surprised.

4NEWGAMES: I can imagine. Most women I've chatted with here are surprised. Actually, I regret that when I have sex with a woman online, I can't see, smell, or taste her. How does she taste? Lick her sweet pussy and let me know how she tastes.

Greg pushed the computer to one side of the bed, spread Mary Kate's legs, and crawled between them.

"Greg, this feels so slutty, somehow."

"Is that bad?" Greg asked, settling between his wife's thighs.

"I guess not. But it's so, so . . . It's like making love with someone watching."

"I find that a real turn-on, but we can sign off anytime you want."

Mary Kate hesitated. "No. It's a turn-on for me, too."

Greg turned his attention to Mary Kate's pussy. He lapped at her soaked skin, exploring every crevice. As he pushed his tongue between her inner lips and penetrated, he held Mary Kate's hips tightly to keep her still. "You taste wonderful." He remained between her legs and reached over to type with one finger.

1SHYGIRL: She tastes spicy and a bit salty. And she's never been so wet.

4NEWGAMES: Feel her pussy. Use one finger and feel everywhere, inside and out. Does she feel different? Is her clit very big and hard? Rub it slowly, all around. And while you do, notice what makes her shiver--what's really good for her. This is making me so hot. I want Mary Kate to type. I'm going to take out my cock and I want her to tell me what she's feeling. It's going to be hard for her to type, but please, do it for me while I stroke myself. I want to share your pleasure.

Mary Kate took the laptop as Greg rubbed and stroked and caressed her cunt. It was hard for her to concentrate on the keyboard, but if NewGames wanted her to type, it was the least she could do. He was teaching them so much about pleasure.

1SHYGIRL: He's touching me. It's hard to type, hard to think about anything but his finger. He's pushing it inside me now and rubbing the walls of my cunt. I want to come, but yet I don't. So good. Are you rubbing yourself, too?

4NEWGAMES: I am. And I'm picturing you and Greg. I love to think about how hot you are. Tell Greg to put two, then three fingers inside you and fuck you with them. While he's doing that, tell him to lick you, too. I want you to come while I'm here.

1SHYGIRL: Yes

Mary Kate was now totally beyond any ability to type. Greg was lapping at her cunt while three fingers moved in and out of her pussy. "Greg, you'll make me come if you keep that up," she groaned.

"Do it. Come baby." He flicked his tongue over her swollen clit.

She did come, screaming one long tone.

Waves of orgasm squeezed Greg's fingers. "I can feel you come," Greg said, amazed. He drew her clit between his lips and sucked while the spasms continued. Later, while Mary Kate quieted, Greg took the laptop.

1SHYGIRL: She came good. It was sensational.

4NEWGAMES: Now it's our turn, Greg. I'm already nude, but you need to strip, too.

1SHYGIRL: Okay

4NEWGAMES: Mary Kate, I want you to do to Greg what I'm doing to my cock.

Breathless, but wanting to bring both Greg and NewGames off, Mary Kate watched the screen. NewGames's responses became much slower.

4NEWGAMES: Hard for me to type now. I'm holding my cock in one hand, rubbing from the tip to my balls.

As Greg lay on the bed, watching the screen, Mary Kate rubbed Greg's cock, following NewGames's instructions.

4NEWGAMES: Now I'm rubbing the fluid that's leaking around the cockhead, and stroking. I'm licking my hand so it's slippery and rubbing up and down. So hard to type. Feels so good. So close. Gonna cum.

Mary Kate licked her hand, then rubbed the full length of Greg's cock. She'd never done anything like this before, but it was wonderful to watch the pleasure on Greg's face. His eyes closed and Mary Kate could see the muscles in his belly tense.

"Now, baby. Squeeze hard and pump."

She did, and Greg came, jets of thick white fluid squirting from the tip and falling onto his chest and belly. "Oh shit," he hissed. "Oh shit."

Mary Kate glanced at the screen and no new words appeared.

When she was confident that Greg was spent, she returned to the keyboard.

1SHYGIRL: Did you come? Greg did, and it was so exciting to watch. I've never done that before.

4NEWGAMES: Yes. I came, too. I was picturing your hand on my cock, Mary Kate, and I came so good.

1SHYGIRL: You can't see my face, but I'm grinning. This was marvelous. Greg's nodding. He liked it, too.

4NEWGAMES: Yes, it was. One thing before we meet again . . .

1SHYGIRL: What?

4NEWGAMES: I think you really must change your screen name. Shy Girl really doesn't apply anymore.

Mary Kate and Greg laughed as she typed, "It really doesn't, does it?"

AGELESS FANTASIES

Everyone at every age has fantasies about everything from telling the boss exactly what to do with his overtime work, to winning the lottery, to being becalmed on a sailboat with Sean Penn or Heather Locklear.

This section and the ones at the ends of the next three chapters contain fantasies that you and your partner can read aloud to get your juices flowing. They cover all sorts of sexual activities, and like all fantasies, are populated by heroes and heroines with perfect bodies who can perform sex flawlessly and frequently. However, this should not prevent you from picturing yourself participating in the exciting things the characters are doing. In fantasies, there are no diseases, no unwanted pregnancies, no past and no future for the characters. Therefore, there is no need for condoms. Would that real life were as kind.

Fantasies are of two types: those that you would actually like to act out and those that are fun to dream about but that you would never consider actually doing. Of course, the line between participation and dreaming differs from person to person, so if your partner bookmarks one of the "Ageless Fantasies" or a story anywhere in this book, be sure you know which group the desire falls into.

Ask your partner for what you want or discuss afterward what might have made the experience even hotter. If you get into a silly situation—and Ed and I have done that often—laugh about it, but keep the warm feelings and continue later. The most important thing is to have fun and not to take it all too seriously.

So grab a bookmark or two, and maybe, with the help of your bookmark, you and your partner can make your fantasies come true someday.

JEFF'S FANTASY

"Excuse me."

Mildly annoyed, Jeff looked up at the man who was trying to get past him in the narrow row of the movie theater.

The movie had started about fifteen minutes earlier. "Why can't these people ever get here on time?" he muttered to himself. "Why do they always have to—"

He stopped abruptly as an astoundingly beautiful woman moved past him in the row, obviously there with the man she followed. She was the most gorgeous thing he had ever seen. She wore a long red T-shirt that came down only a few inches below her perfectly formed ass. Jeff could have sworn that she wasn't wearing anything beneath.

As she moved past, she turned and looked at him. "Thank you," she said as she and her companion moved to the center of the row. Her date wasted no time putting his arm around her, pulling her close.

Jeff couldn't take his eyes off her. His whole world had become the beauty in red seated several tantalizing feet to his left. The movie was good, and pretty sexy for an R-rated film, but since the film was several months old, the theater was only about one-third full. There was no one else in the row besides Jeff, the woman, and her date.

Jeff started fantasizing about the woman in the red T-shirt, imagining what he would do to her if she was his woman. He imagined slowly stripping her and tying her spread-eagled to his bed while he used his tongue to explore every nook and cranny of her body, tantalizing and teasing her until she begged him to fuck her. He might refuse at first, make her beg some more, but eventually he would fuck her. He'd fuck her long and hard, over and over again. He'd be the best fuck she had ever had. The fantasy was so good and so real that, absently, his hand dropped down to his crotch, where, without his even realizing it, he began to brush his hand lightly across his now-bulging cock. With the flimsy shorts he was wearing, the lump in his lap was painfully apparent. He stared at the screen and slipped away.

As he stroked his cock in the darkened theater, the woman in red caught his movement out of the corner of her eye and turned her head slightly to look. Their eyes locked momentarily and she smiled. Suddenly realizing what he was doing, Jeff quickly moved his hand and turned a deep shade of red. It's a good thing it's dark in here, he thought. Maybe she didn't notice.

But she had noticed, and the sight had turned her on. Moving her date's arm, which had been draped around her since the movie started, she placed his hand on her thigh, about midway up, just at the hem of the long red shirt. Jeff could just barely hear her purr as she leaned over and licked her date's ear.

Jeff watched in amazement as she started slowly rubbing her legs together, silently signaling that she was horny and willing. The man started stroking her thigh, moving his hand up and down the smooth expanse of her flesh. She responded by parting her legs just a little, encouraging him to go farther. She reached over and put her hand in her date's lap, squeezing his hard dick through his pants.

Unable to believe what he was seeing, Jeff forgot completely about the movie and stared at the private show that was playing out for him several seats over. Once again, he placed his hand in his lap, more openly now, and massaged his massive erection. The woman looked over again, licked her lips, and winked in approval.

It was obvious to Jeff that the woman was getting hotter and hotter, and bolder and bolder, and Jeff was sure one of the ushers was going to see them and throw them out. But, amazingly, he seemed to be the only one who noticed. The woman parted her legs even farther and sat up slightly, allowing the man next to her to pull the shirt up above her waist, exposing her neatly trimmed pussy. As Jeff had guessed, she was not wearing any panties. Jeff could see her moist cunt glistening in the dark auditorium, and he imagined what it would be like to be between her legs, sucking and licking her hard, sensitive clit.

The man touched her wet pussy, eliciting a tiny gasp from the woman, who was trying her best to be silent and unobtrusive. Jeff watched her nipples harden under her shirt, and he could almost taste her breasts in his waiting mouth. Jeff's erection was rock-hard now, begging to be freed and stroked. Should he? Or would that ruin the moment?

In the bright light from the movie screen, Jeff could see the man insert his middle finger into the woman's cunt. She arched her back and gasped for air, surprised by the suddenness of his act. In and out he pumped, while she moved, just slightly, with each stroke.

Reaching up, she squeezed her right breast, pinching her nipple and making it even harder. She glanced over at Jeff and, noticing his obvious approval, smiled. She obviously enjoyed the audience.

Suddenly, she tensed, and Jeff could tell that she was coming. Her open mouth betrayed the scream that would have ripped from her throat had they not been in public. Taking only a moment to catch her breath, she bent over, putting her head in her date's lap, and started kissing his dick. This was more than Jeff could take, and he pulled his shorts back, just barely exposing the head of his throbbing cock. This is crazy, Jeff thought. What if I get caught? But he was too far gone to care.

Then Jeff heard a zipping sound, and he looked over, to see the woman freeing the man's blood-engorged tool from his pants. The man's head was back, eyes closed, obviously not caring that he was in a public place. Purring quietly, the woman in red started at the base, slid her tongue up the length of his cock, then circled the head teasingly. She kissed it several times before putting just the head in her waiting mouth. Jeff watched as she stroked her date's cock while sucking the head.

Jeff couldn't control himself anymore. Fully taking his erect cock from his shorts, he began to pump and stroke it furiously. He, too, had lost track of where he was, and he could see only the couple next to him. She moved around in her seat so that he could see her beautiful, round ass and her wet, juicy cunt. Jeff watched her head bob up and down on her date's cock as the man's hands gripped the back of her head.

She reached down between her legs with one hand and started stroking her glistening cunt, her fingers flying faster and faster the closer her man got to orgasm. Suddenly, the man tensed, trying his best to stifle a scream, obviously filling her mouth with semen. She plunged three fingers into her pussy and Jeff could see her lips contracting as she came again. At the same time, Jeff came, turning slightly so that several drops of fluid fell on her beautiful ass. The man sat with his head thrown back, totally spent. The woman rested her head in his lap, and with one finger, she wiped a drop of Jeff's come off her ass and, slowly, seductively, brought it to her lips. She extended her tongue and, with the tip, licked Jeff's come from her fingers. "Mmm," Jeff heard her purr. He knew that she had enjoyed giving the show as much as he had enjoyed watching it.

Suddenly, Jeff was aware that the credits were rolling up the screen. He had missed almost the entire movie while dreaming about the woman in the red T-shirt. He looked to his left and saw a row of empty seats. No woman, with or without a red T-shirt. Not that he would have done anything even if he could have, he realized. He was a happily married man. But anyone could fantasize.

He thought of his wife of almost two years, who was arriving home from a business trip later that evening, and smiled. He would meet her at the airport, and then, when they got home . . .

CHARLOTTE'S FANTASY

Charlotte loved romance novels. She read at least two a week and enjoyed nothing more than curling up with a book on a winter afternoon while her husband watched sports on TV. After reading one particularly erotic scene, she found herself gazing off into space.

Charlotte ran across the dark yard toward the gazebo, where she knew Armand would be waiting. Not even noticing the sultry Louisiana heat, she lifted her hooped skirt and felt the dew-dampened grass soak her silk slippers as she sped away from the music and rich food and revelers in the mansion behind her. No one must see me, she thought, looking over her shoulder. Good. No one.

About fifty feet from the gazebo, she slowed, then stopped and tried to catch her breath. Was she breathless from running or from the expectation of Armand's muscular arms, lean body, and handsome face? He would be her husband in a few weeks, but, except for a few minutes at the party thrown in their honor, she hadn't seen him in almost a month.

"I'm here, darling," the husky voice said.

A smile lighting her face, she lifted her hoop skirt higher and ran to the gazebo, to Armand. She climbed the three steps and almost threw herself into her fiancé's arms. "Oh Armand," she whispered. "This is so dangerous. We shouldn't be alone like this. What would Papa and Mama say?"

"I couldn't bear to watch you from a distance, looking at you politely, telling everyone how much I am looking forward to our wedding." He closed his arms tightly around her and buried his face in her hair. "Oh darling, I wanted to hold you, to touch you, to love you."

Charlotte turned her face up to his and felt his lips brush hers. "Oh yes," she whispered against his mouth.

He pressed his lips more tightly against hers and rubbed his tongue against their joining. "Open for me, pet. Let me taste you."

Tentatively, as she had done a few times before, she parted her lips and let his tongue plunder her mouth's depths. They kissed for long moments, and Charlotte felt heat flow over her. She pulled back, withdrew a lacy handkerchief from her cleavage, and blotted her chest. "Oh my dear sir," she said, "you do know how to kiss me."

"I want so much more," Armand said, taking the handkerchief and brushing it gently across her chest. The neckline of Charlotte's dress was so low that he could almost see the tops of her areolas. He brushed the lace deeply into her cleavage, admiring the luscious globes on either side.

"Sir," Charlotte simpered playfully, "we mustn't."

"And why not?" Armand said. "In two weeks, we'll be married. We'll be able to do whatever we want. Why must we wait?"

"We just have to."

Armand dipped his fingers into the deep valley between her breasts and caressed her damp skin. With a quick flick of his fingers, he found her nipple and lifted it from the confines of her bodice. He pinched the swollen bud, then dipped his face and licked. Feeling her tremble, he placed his forearm against the small of her back, pressed her closer to his body, and suckled. "You want this," he purred, his breath tickling her wet, erect nipple.

He took advantage of her silence to lift the other breast from its fabric nest and bite the tip. "You want this," he repeated. When she didn't respond, he placed his other arm behind her knees and lifted her into his arms, then sat on the bench of the gazebo, with her on his lap.

In the light of the full moon, Charlotte could see the glow of the white of Armand's shirt between the sides of his black jacket. Beneath her hand, she could feel the strong, rapid beat of his heart. She looked at his shadowed face and saw his smile. Yes, she did want him. But she couldn't admit that. And she certainly couldn't have more than a few stolen kisses—not until they were married. She touched his beautiful mouth and he nipped her finger.

While he played with her finger, he placed his hand on her silk-covered ankle. "Your skin is so soft," he whispered, sliding his hand up her calf, finding the bare skin above her stockings.

"You mustn't," she said, her breathing quickening.

Ignoring her protests, he slid his hand higher, up the inside of her pantalet-covered thigh. "I just want to touch you." The hand slipped higher, toward the split in the fabric.

"But Armand . . ." She tried to move away from the questing fingers but only succeeded in allowing him further liberties. As she knew he would, his fingers found the hot, wet center of her hunger. She wanted to stop him. She knew she must. But it felt so good, that finger, rubbing and probing. She had never felt anything like this. "Armand . . ." She wanted, needed—but what?

"I know, my love. Let me show you how good it will be when we are married."

He seemed to know how to feed the hunger. His finger rubbing her center, his mouth dipping to suckle at her breast. Rubbing, sucking. Pulling her toward something. Pulling. Pulling. Her body was unable to resist the pull. But she must try. Mustn't she? Finally, she stopped resisting and let her hips move with a life of their own.

He sensed the moment she surrendered to him. Smiling, he moved her slightly, just enough to allow him to unfasten the front of his britches and let his hard cock spring free. With a sweep of cotton, he lifted Charlotte so she straddled him, his cock aimed at her heat. "Darling, I wish we had a soft feather bed where I could love you properly, but we both need this now. And we must eventually return to the party. Tell me you want this as much as I do."

Charlotte sighed into the hot night. "Yes," she whispered. "I do want you. Please."

"There will be a little pain, but I will make it as easy for you as I can. After the pain, darling, I will never hurt you again." He lifted her with his strong arms and, buried beneath her skirts and petticoats, his cock found her. With a sudden upthrust, he drove himself inside of her.

She felt a moment of pain, then the hunger began to build anew. His hands found her under the cotton. One hand held her tightly against him, the other forced its way between their bodies to her now-erect clit. He rubbed again, and as he felt her tighten, he pressed his mouth against hers.

She was reaching for it, whatever it was, reaching for what that finger was pushing her toward. Lights. Shards of colored lights. Closer and closer, tightening her thighs and low in her belly. Suddenly, the lights burst and showered her with brilliant stars. She wanted to scream against his mouth, but Armand kept his lips tightly against hers, preventing her cries. She felt him tighten, then arch his back and thrust upward, more deeply into her heat. Pulses of power flowed from him into her.

When they had quieted, he helped her to clean herself, then righted himself and his clothing. "Oh Armand," she said softly. "I never imagined. Is it always like that?"

"And better. So much better."

As she calmed, she heard the sounds of the Louisiana night mixed with the distant music. She smelled the damp smell of the nearby bayou, felt the rough texture of Armand's jacket. It all seemed new and fresh, as if this experience had sharpened her senses. And it could be better?

Later, hand in hand, not totally able to conceal the ravages of lovemaking, the two lovers walked back toward the house.

Charlotte sighed, looked up, and saw her husband staring down at her, that special look in his eye. "Where in the world were you?" he asked.

"Just dreaming," Charlotte answered. "Is the game over?"

"No," he said, "but I've been dreaming myself. I'm wondering what you're doing for the next hour or so."

Charlotte grinned. "Why," she said coyly, "did you have something particular in mind?"

He grinned down at her, then placed one hand on each arm of her chair, trapping her. "Actually, several somethings."

Charlotte grabbed the front of his sweater and pulled until he dropped on top of her into the chair. "Good," she said, "me, too."

3.
Now We Have Children

A father and his four-year-old son were walking through the park one afternoon and they happened upon a male dog mounting a female dog.

"What are they doing?" the little boy asked.

The father hadn't yet thought through the matter of introducing his son to the mysteries of sex. So honestly, if a bit hesitantly, the father answered, "Why, they're making puppies."

"Oh," the small boy said.

A few nights later, the boy walked into his parents' bedroom, intending to ask for a drink of water. He saw his mother and father, belly-to-belly, doing what mommies and daddies do late at night.

"Whatcha doing, Daddy?" he asked.

With only a moment's hesitation, the father answered, "We're making babies, son."

"Turn her over, Daddy," the boy yelled. "I want puppies."

I don't think it will come as a surprise to anyone that living with children may be the largest obstacle to a couple's sexual fulfillment. Somehow lovemaking appears on the priority list somewhere below shopping, cooking, laundry, cleaning, helping the kids with their homework and only slightly above removing the crabgrass from the front lawn.

"Darling," he says, nibbling on the back of his wife's neck, "I've been thinking about you all day. How about going to bed a bit early tonight?"

"Oh sweetheart, I'd love to," she says, turning in his arms. "But you still haven't folded the laundry, and I need to bake twenty-seven cupcakes for Jennifer's kindergarten class." She glances at her watch. "It's almost nine-thirty. We won't get to bed before eleven."

"I know," he says, yawning. "And the alarm goes off at five of six tomorrow morning. Maybe this weekend."

Sound familiar?

Books and articles on sexual health urge people to work hard at sex during these stressful years. "Sure, right," she says. "I'm willing to try. But I work all day, take care of kids, shop, clean, and now you want me to put on a sexy negligee and seduce my husband. All I want to do is sleep."

Then he says, "I commute an hour each way to and from work, bust my butt to earn a decent living and support the kids. Now I'm supposed to bring her flowers and wine?"

She says, "I used to feel like a sex object. Now I'm a typist and a mommy and there's not much time for anything else."

He says, "At first, my wife was passionate. Now

she's disinterested, thinking more about the kids than about me. I'm just a wage earner."

Finally, you manage to find time, energy, and desire for lovemaking. You're in bed, stroking and recalling when you were lovers instead of parents. Then a voice says, "Mommy, I don't feel too well," or "Daddy, I had a bad dream." Oh well . . .

And the problems don't end when the children reach school age. It can feel awkward to make love with the kids still up, watching TV or listening to music. "What if they hear us? They'll know what we're doing." Embarrassing, isn't it?

Before we get to specifics, let's get one thing straight. If you don't make an effort to keep the flame alive despite the children, you won't have any quality sex with your partner until the kids are in college. And, for me at least, the longer I went without good sex, or even sex at all, the less I wanted it. I seemed to forget how nice it had been and I decided that I could easily do without.

The good news is this: It really is possible to feel less like mommies and daddies and more like lovers, even in a house that's filled with toys, basketballs, and computer games. Let's consider the problems with the children and try to find some short- or long-term solutions. Many of these will seem simplistic, and some are. But relax and think seriously about some of these ideas, even though at first blush they might seem awkward.

Couples frequently overlook the need to set aside time for sex. They make time for relatives, for business dinners, for painting the guest room. If they get tickets for the hottest show in town, they hire a baby-sitter

and find the energy. Seldom, however, do they make
a date with each other for Saturday night.

So do it. Make a date with your husband or wife.
Pick a day and time and then stick to it. No changing
at the last minute because Susie has a runny nose or
Andy needs help with his algebra.

Then line up a baby-sitter. If no baby-sitter is available or affordable, arrange with grandparents, cousins,
friends, or neighbors to take care of the kids for the
entire evening. If you can find a way, make plans for
someone to stay with your children all night, or, better
still, take them to that person's house until the following day. Trade an evening of caring for your neighbors' kids for an evening of them taking yours. Your
neighbors probably need an evening alone just as
much as you two do.

Next, anticipate the evening the way you did when
you were dating. Tease each other with little notes
about what you're going to do that evening. Try not to
let your mind lose the delicious anxiety. The morning
of the "big evening," tie a string around your partner's
wrist as a reminder, so that every time he or she looks
down, the vision of you naked and willing will appear.

Wear something special. Dressed in the same old
jeans and shirt, you are the same old mommy or
daddy. Dress up for a change, as if it's a special occa-
sion, because it is! Buy something new, or borrow
something sexy from a friend. Take whatever time you
can scrounge and enjoy a shower. Wouldn't it be nice
to take a bubble bath? (I'm not going to press my luck
here.) Use a new cologne or a new shampoo. Use
hand lotion. Find a tape of the music the two of you
used to listen to when you were dating and put it into
the player in the car.

Have a relaxed dinner at an intimate restaurant and then rent a room at a fancy hotel or the local Super 8, even if it's just for an hour. Share a bath and make love in front of the bathroom mirror. Make as much noise as you like. Make love with the lights on. Make love more than once, slowly.

With two small children, Alice and Tim had neither the time nor the energy to spend on themselves, even though they had enough money. After more than a year, they finally decided to make time for long, leisurely loving. And when they did, the results were delightful.

ALICE AND TIM'S STORY

Alice and Tim had twin fifteen-month-old girls. The twins were gorgeous, smart, good eaters, and easy sleepers. Alice and Tim, however, were exhausted. An accountant, Tim worked long hours to get ahead, and Alice spent her days changing diapers, feeding babies, and never getting a moment's peace. By the time Tim got home and they all had dinner, bathed the babies, and got them down for the night, both parents were ready for bed and sleep—just sleep. Once a week or so, they indulged in a quickie, which left them feeling briefly physically satisfied but emotionally empty.

"You know, baby," Tim said one evening as they collapsed into bed, "I miss making love. Long, luxurious, caressing, touching, hugging, kissing love."

"I know. Me, too. I remember it well, and I'm sure it used to be lots of fun." Alice yawned.

"How about asking your folks to baby-sit while they're here next weekend?"

"Oh Tim. My folks don't get much chance to see us, and they only have this long weekend."

"I know, but I want to spend an evening with you. Just you."

Alice yawned again. "I'll see whether I'm comfortable asking."

The following afternoon, Alice called her mother, who lived about four hundred miles away. "Mom," she said in the middle of the conversation, "I was wondering whether you and Dad might baby-sit with the twins one evening so Tim and I can have dinner together, just the two of us."

Her mother's warm voice jumped in quickly. "Of course, dear. We planned to do that all along as a surprise. We thought you could go out Saturday evening. We'll feed the girls so you two can do something fun for a change. And we'll even take the baby monitor so you won't be bothered until morning."

Alice shared the good news with Tim that evening and Tim agreed to make all the arrangements. Since it would be a surprise, Tim told Alice only that she should dress up in a very fancy outfit and be ready at six o'clock sharp.

Late Saturday afternoon, Alice and Tim got dressed, hugged the girls and Alice's parents, and walked out the front door. There, parked at the curb, was the longest limousine Alice had ever seen. "Tim, is that for us?"

"It certainly is. Nothing but the best."

"But a limo? That's so expensive."

"I want to be able to drink and get a little blitzed tonight without having to worry about driving home. So I thought this was the best idea."

At the sight of the couple, the limo driver trotted around the car and opened the door. The couple climbed in and found a chilled bottle of champagne and two glasses. On the way downtown, they sipped the bubbly liquid and giggled as if they were two teenagers on their way to the prom.

The restaurant was packed, but, thanks to Tim's reservation, they were seated and served efficiently. By the end of the main course, the couple had finished most of a bottle of wine Tim had selected and were relaxed and happy. "Remember that evening we had dinner at that seafood place at the beach?" Tim asked.

Alice remembered it well and flushed.

"Would you do that again?" Tim asked.

Alice well remembered that she had gone into the ladies' room and taken off her underwear. "Oh Timmy." She giggled.

"Do it. For me."

Alice walked to the ladies' room. Glad she had worn a soft silk blouse and tight skirt, she entered a stall and took off her bra and panties. Wearing only a garter belt, stockings, and a slip beneath her clothes, she returned to the table. Tim placed his hand, palm up, on the table. Blushing, Alice placed her undergarments in his hand.

"That's a good girl," Tim said, slipping the clothing into his jacket pocket and moving beside her on the banquette. Beneath the overhang of the tablecloth, he squeezed Alice's knee, then slid her skirt up. As the waiter took their dessert orders, Tim slid the tips of his fingers up the inside of her thigh and felt her shiver. With a bit of wiggling, his fingers reached her soaking pussy and he flicked his finger over her clit.

Trying to look relaxed, Alice moved slightly and

pressed her thighs together. "Timmy, please," she said breathlessly.

Tim leaned over and blew a stream of cool air down the front of her blouse and watched her nipples tighten. "I can see your hard little nippies through that material," he whispered. "Does that embarrass you?"

"You know it does," Alice said, her cheeks flushed.

"Good."

While the two lovers ate their dessert, Tim frequently reached beneath Alice's skirt and played with her pussy. By the time Tim had paid the check, Alice was trembling with need. "I don't want to go home," she whined.

"And we won't," Tim said, pulling a room key for the hotel next door from his pocket. He glanced at his watch. "It's almost nine. The limo is due at eleven, but the driver said he'd wait as long as we needed." Tim grinned. "He's got three kids under ten and is thrilled to help us with this evening together."

"You do think of everything, baby," Alice said, hugging Tim's arm.

In the hotel room, Alice found another bottle of Chardonnay chilling. "When did you set this all up?"

"I picked up the key earlier this afternoon when I took your dad to the supermarket."

"You mean my father knows about this?"

"He suggested the wine."

"Dirty old man." Alice grinned.

Tim grabbed for Alice and nibbled at her lips. "Yup. He and your mom seem to have it real good." He gazed at his wife admiringly. Then he reached over and turned on the radio and tuned it to an easy-listening station. "Remember how you used to dance for me?"

"Ummm." Alice smiled, then extended her arms

horizontally and swayed her hips. She danced around the room while Tim poured wine. He settled himself on the bed. "Would you do a strip for me?"

Alice winked at him, then slowly unbuttoned the top button of her blouse. It took four songs before the blouse was open to her waist. Without a bra for support, her breasts swayed, and Tim caught a glimpse of her smoky nipples. Alice wiggled her shoulders close to him, but when he reached for her, she slapped his hands away. "Patience, baby," she purred.

With agonizing deliberation, she unzipped her skirt and pulled it and her half-slip off. Dressed in her unbuttoned blouse, garter belt, and stockings, she moved around the room, watching the lust build in her husband's eyes. Alice turned her back to Tim to remove her blouse teasingly. She saw that she was reflected in the wide mirror over the dresser. "Can you see me?" she asked, noticing Tim's gaze shift to the mirror. She let the blouse slide off her shoulders and fall to the floor. Then she cupped her breasts and leaned forward.

The combination of the wine and the erotic atmosphere made Alice a bit more daring than she might otherwise have been. She leaned against the mirror and pressed her nipples against the cold glass. "Ooh," she crooned. "Feels cold." She watched Tim almost leap off the bed and come up behind her.

"Watch me in the mirror," he said, standing against her back and holding her hands in his. "See how we both hold your breasts?" Alice slumped against him and they both watched his dark, hairy hands play with her white breasts. Slowly, he slid his hands down her belly and into her bush.

"You're still all dressed," Alice said, turning and

quickly removing her husband's shirt, slacks, and underwear. "That's better."

Tim cupped her buttocks and lifted her so she sat on the dresser, her back against the cold glass of the mirror. He spread her legs wide, stepped between them, and pulled her forward so her hot pussy was against the tip of his rock-hard penis. "You asked for this, baby." He pulled her toward him and buried his cock in her cunt.

"Oh baby. Fuck me good."

Tim pulled back, then slowly inserted his cock again. In and out, slowly and deliberately, he alternately filled and emptied Alice's cunt. When he withdrew again, Alice wrapped her hand around his hard, wet shaft and squeezed. As he pushed forward, she let his cock slide slowly through her fist and into her waiting pussy. As she cupped his balls, he pounded. "Not yet," she yelled. "Just a moment." She twined her legs around his waist, linked her feet, and held him tightly inside. Panting, she felt her climax slowly wash over her, then thunder through her entire body. "Now," she screamed, and Tim let his orgasm take him.

They dozed, then made love again. They returned to their limo just before midnight and arrived home to a darkened house. As they walked toward their bedroom, Alice whispered, "You know Mom and Dad have the monitor. No one will disturb us until morning."

Tim nipped at her earlobe. "How about if I disturb you?"

"Yeah," she said. "How about that."

Of course, you can't always go out to make love like Alice and Tim did, and no couple can afford a trip to some hotel every time the mood strikes them. So it's necessary to make your home a place where all kinds of loving, from hugging and hand-holding to wild chandelier-swinging, take place frequently.

"Okay," you mutter, "how do I do that? After all, I have kids, and they're smart little devils."

I have several suggestions.

First, and most important, as soon as they can understand, teach your children that when Mommy and Daddy's door is closed, they have to knock. Tell them that you will respond to their needs but that you need some time alone and they're not to snoop. And do the same for them. Knock on their door when it's closed, as well. If you don't respect their privacy, they will not learn to respect yours.

Second, put a hook and eye on your door to keep the inquisitive and forgetful from wandering in at the worst moment, like the little boy in the story at the beginning of this chapter. And put it high enough that the children can't reach it and lock themselves in.

Third, when you and your partner want some time together, tell the children that Mommy and Daddy want to kiss and hug and love in private. Psychologists agree that children are comforted by the fact that Mommy and Daddy love each other and want to spend time together. Children talk to their friends, most of whom have more than a passing acquaintance with divorce; deep inside, most children think about it and wonder whether it can, in fact, happen in their family. So don't hesitate to act loving where the kids can see. Don't force it if it doesn't feel comfortable, but if you want to touch, do it. If you want to kiss your spouse on the back of the neck, do that, too. And do the same with your children so Mommy and Daddy's loving is part of the natural way things work.

I remember overhearing a conversation between one of my children and a friend at the age of about five.

My daughter had just finished telling her friend what she had done the previous evening. Her friend responded, "Mom and I got a new videotape from the library after school yesterday, so she sent me to my room to watch it. Mommy and Daddy told me they were watching TV, again." She gave a strange inflection to the last word, which my daughter caught, too.

"Again?" she asked.

"Yeah. They go in their room, turn the TV up real loud, and giggle. They really think I don't know they're kissing and tickling each other."

"Oh," my daughter said. That evening, she asked me what I thought her friend's parents were doing. I told her in short sentences about loving, hugging, kissing, and a little about lovemaking. After each very short explanation, I made it clear that she could ask additional questions if she wanted to, until she reached the end of her curiosity and patience, which she did quickly.

By the way, on the subject of telling children about sex, here's an old story that emphasizes the need for making sure you answer the questions your child is asking.

A seven-year-old boy was riding in the car with his father.

"Dad," the boy said, "where did I come from?"

Dad struggled with the pros and cons of telling his son about sex, then decided that since they had a long trip ahead of them, there would never be a better time. He spent half an hour on his explanation, barely pausing for breath. Finally, he said, "Well, son, does that explain it for you?"

"Well, Dad, that was really interesting, but, well, Davie says he came from Denver. I just wondered where I came from."

Enough said.

Some couples with small children have, unfortunately for their sex life, gotten in the habit of letting Junior sleep in their bed.

Let's say Junior is a boy, and since his bouts with night terrors as a baby, you've let him continue either to go to sleep in your bed or to creep in during the night. Plays hell with your sex life, doesn't it? Well, unless there's a special reason, such as illness or severe space constraints, most child psychologists agree that children don't belong in Mommy and Daddy's bed. Therefore, it's time to get him used to his own bed—full-time.

Americans put a very strong emphasis on privacy and on sexuality. It is true that in other cultures, people share beds, rooms, and the like in a normal, natural way. But we aren't living in other cultures.

I listen to a radio psychologist, a very down-to-earth, sensible lady. A caller recently phoned her and said, "My son comes to bed with my husband and me every night. I know I have to get him back in his own bed. How mean should I be?" The psychologist's reply was very sensible: "Think of it as 'firm,' not 'mean,' and you'll feel a lot better about it." That makes a lot of sense. Take Junior to the store and get him his own personal flashlight, a night-light, a sleeping bag, whatever his choice is to ease the transition. Then explain that Mommy and Daddy sleep in their bed and he sleeps in his. And that's the way it will work from now on. Then be prepared! You will probably have to put up with several nights of screaming. You may need to get a lock for your door. Junior will pound on your door and shriek for a while, possibly all night. But every time you give in and let him into your room and into your bed, you will have to begin all over again, and it will be even more difficult the next time.

A man is doing a survey about the varied household uses of Vaseline. He knocks on one door and a rather harried-looking woman answers. She agrees to answer his questions. After several inquiries, he finally asks, "Do you use Vaseline during sex?"

"Yes," she answers.

"Does the male partner or the female partner use it?"

"Oh," she says, "neither. We put it on the doorknob so the kids can't come in."

After I told this joke to a dear friend of mine, she told me the story of her recent adventures with her seven-year-old daughter, whom we'll call Lisa. Lisa enjoyed climbing into bed with Mommy and Daddy, but this late-night practice was putting a crimp in their sex life. So my friend and her husband had made the difficult decision to bar the child from the bedroom. They put a better lock on the bedroom door and waited for the storm.

About eleven that evening, Lisa knocked on the door and then, on being told that she should go back to bed, threw a fit. She banged on the door, kicked, and cried. After a few minutes, suddenly there was silence, followed by rustling sounds outside the door. As the parents debated what might be going on, time passed.

Five minutes later, to my friends' astonishment, the door flew open. In walked the seven-year-old, the doorknob in one hand and a screwdriver in the other. I sympathized with my friend's dilemma: whether to chastise the girl for disobeying, praise her for her ingenuity, or merely laugh. When my friend told me this tale, we decided that Lisa has a brilliant future, either as a rocket scientist or a cat burglar.

A suggestion: Don't waste any small flicker of sensuality. You don't have the luxury of saying, "This isn't the best moment. I'll resist this temptation and wait till a better, more convenient moment." There are no convenient moments. If you want to make love and it's at all possible, do it. Jill found such a moment and decided not to let it pass.

JILL AND TONY'S STORY

T.J. was eight months old. Colicky since birth, he had one or the other of his parents awake just about every night. Because T.J. was now on soy formula and not breast milk, Tony and Jill alternated the middle-of-the-night feedings and soothings. This night, it had been Jill's turn.

As she sat with little T.J. lying facedown across her thighs, Jill idly rubbed his back and thought about Tony. How long had it been, she mused, since they had made long, luxurious love? Weeks? Months? As she felt her impatience rising, she forced it down. That won't do any good at all, she told herself. I want him. I miss him. But what can I do about it?

As T.J. fell asleep, Jill found her body tingling at the memories of the delicious times she and Tony had spent together before T.J.'s birth. She remembered their spontaneous lovemaking, once in the car, pulled over on the parkway, once in the woods when they slipped away from a family picnic. God, those were good, she thought, lifting a sleeping T.J. into his crib.

As she slipped from the room, she became aware of the wetness between her legs. She was hungry for Tony and just had to find the best way to make lovemaking happen. She could wake him up right away. But that wasn't quite what she had in mind.

As she reentered the master bedroom, she saw that Tony was sprawled on the bed, arms and legs spread wide. Since he slept nude and the moon was bright, she was able to gaze at the body that still excited her after five years of marriage. As she stared at his flaccid penis, she smiled slowly. She usually enjoyed oral sex, but recently there had been little time to indulge. This was too much of a temptation to resist.

She peeled off her nightgown and gently settled herself on the bed beside Tony, not disturbing his sound sleep. She scooted down until her head was at the level of his hip. Then she leaned over and touched the tip of her tongue to the velvety skin of his soft cock. So smooth, she thought. So tasty. She licked slowly from base to tip, watching the organ move of its own accord.

She licked again, and she was amazed at how quickly it began to grow, but still Tony didn't move. How much can I do before he wakes up? she wondered. How hard can I make him?

She licked gently, over and over, frequently blowing on the wet area. When Tony's cock was semihard, she licked the tip, then wrapped her lips around the head and created a slight suction with her cheeks. Ever so slowly, she drew the cock into her mouth, sliding her tongue over the underside. Never able to "deep-throat," she could only get about half of the now-engorged cock into her mouth. Slowly, keeping a slight vacuum in her mouth, she drew back, and Tony's cock pulled from her mouth until only the tip remained inside.

Still he didn't move. In and out she sucked his penis, enjoying the freedom to get used to the feel of it in her mouth, the taste of the drops of fluid that soon oozed from the tip, the smell of his groin. Then, while Tony's cock was inside of her mouth, she used her fingers to stroke his balls.

"Do that for another minute and I'll come in your mouth," Tony said, his voice raspy with passion.

With his cock still in her mouth, Jill looked up at her husband through her lashes. It came as a surprise to her that although she had never let him come in her mouth before, she wanted him to do just that. She wanted to be able to experience his orgasm fully. While flicking the tip of her tongue over the tip of Tony's cock, Jill stroked the tender area between the base of his scrotum and his anus.

"Do you know what you're doing?" Tony gasped. She could feel the tension in his entire body. He was trying to control the urge to release.

"Hmm," she hummed, the sound vibrating through his body. "Hmm." She knew the exact moment when he gave in and let his body respond. His hips bucked and suddenly she felt her mouth fill with thick, slightly tangy fluid. She couldn't swallow it, so she released the tight seal on his cock and let the goo pour over his balls. Spurt after spurt of semen dribbled from her lips and she reveled in the joy she felt, giving so much pleasure to her husband.

When his body quieted, she pulled back and placed her head on his belly.

"What brought that on?" Tony said, out of breath.

"I have no idea," Jill answered. "It was just something I wanted to do, so I did it."

"You can't imagine how glad I am that you did."

Jill lifted her head and looked at her husband. "By the way, how long had you been awake?"

"For a while. But I was being selfish, I know. It felt so good, and I was afraid that if I let you know I was awake, you'd stop."

Jill smiled. "I did give you pleasure, didn't I?"

Tony grabbed Jill under her arms and pulled her up beside him. "Baby, you have no idea." As she cuddled against him, he felt her hard nipples rub against his side. "You know, I can show you just how much." He pushed her onto her back. "Close your eyes and pretend to be asleep." He spread her legs wide apart.

"Hmm," Jill purred, then made a few fake snoring sounds. Jill and Tony didn't get back to sleep for an hour.

We all know that it's hard to con a kid. They are usually smarter than any of us. Since I love stories about children, I thought I'd slip one more in as an example of how difficult it is to get anything past our progeny.

● ● ●

One afternoon, a six-year-old boy approached his mother. "Mom," he asked, "how old are you?"

"Son," she explained, "there are some questions that it isn't polite to ask any woman, even your mother."

"Oh," he said. "Okay, how much do you weigh?"

The mother chuckled. "You know, honey, you've just found one of the only other questions it's really impolite to ask anyone."

"Oh," he said again.

"You're full of questions today," the mother said. "Maybe you have one I can answer."

"Mom, why did Dad move out?"

"Well, son, we decided it's better for us to live apart for a while. I'll explain more about this sort of thing when you're older."

"Okay."

As the six-year-old left the kitchen, he was accosted by his eight-year-old brother. "You don't have to ask her that stuff," the brother said. "Let's get her driver's license. It's all on there."

A few minutes later, the six-year-old returned to the kitchen. "Mom, I know everything."

"You do?" the mother said.

"Yes. I know you're thirty-three years old and you weigh one hundred and twenty-nine pounds. And I know why Dad left, too."

"Oh? Why was that?"

"You got an F in sex."

TRY SOMETHING NEW:
CONTROL GAMES

Many people have fantasies that involve either being in complete control of a sexual situation or giving up control to their partner. The captive of the swashbuckling pirate, the victim of the clever temptress, the prisoner in a dungeon. And these stories aren't limited to the man wanting control and the woman wanting to surrender. Dominant women figure in both male and female fantasies.

The ultimate control fantasy is the dream rape—a woman being subdued by a handsome, considerate, yet totally overpowering stranger and forced to endure and enjoy all the forbidden things he does to her body. And, during the fantasy rape, she finds she cannot help but become excited. This fantasy rape forms the basis of many of the scenes from books and movies, the most famous being the scene in which Rhett carries Scarlett, kicking and screaming, up the wide stairs to the bedroom.

I don't intend to get into any psychobabble here about why these exist or whether they indicate some severe problem in childhood. I will say only this: I've played both the submissive and dominant roles with my partner and I find both tremendously enjoyable. And I had a well-balanced, healthy childhood.

Irrespective of where they originate, control fantasies exist and can be some of the most erotic to act out with your partner. If you've never tried being in complete control, or surrendering complete control, open your mind and read on. Of course, if these fantasies are a turnoff for you and you have no thought of ever trying even a mild version of control, skip to the next section.

What's the lure of the control fantasy?

The controller is free to do whatever he wants, and/or to "force" his partner to do whatever he wants done to his body.

The controllee is freed from the responsibility of pleasing her partner. She doesn't have to worry about whether she's doing the right thing.

A warning: In order to act out any control fantasy, several ground rules must be established from the outset. Control fantasies must never be used to force anyone to do anything that is even mildly repugnant. Period. In order to assure that both parties are in complete agreement, safe words must be used and the rules adhered to at all times by both parties.

A safe word is an agreed-upon word or phrase that means "Stop. Now!" Why, you are asking, can't one partner just use the word *stop*? I can tell you from experience that saying, "Stop, please stop," and knowing that your partner won't, is wonderfully liberating. It's another way of reinforcing that you've surrendered control.

So decide on an unusual word that will mean "Stop, now!" to both partners—maybe *mustard* or *crankcase*. Many couples use two words, *red* for "Stop now!" and *yellow* for "Stop for a moment; my foot's asleep."

Once you've agreed on the safe words, both of you must agree on how they are to be used. The one in control must agree that the use of this word means to stop immediately and that, if it is used, he will do exactly that—immediately and without hesitation or blame. Mutual trust is an imperative. If you don't trust your partner to stop when you say so, or to say "Stop" when he or she wants to, don't play.

The one who is to be controlled must agree to use the word if things get the least bit uncomfortable. This isn't an endurance contest, and the controllee must never let things continue "just" to please a partner. Consider that if you do, or have done to you, something you hate, it will be a long time before you will get into that situation again. So much for the frequency of sex.

An agreement to use a safe word frees both partners. The one in control can now do anything—and I do mean *anything*—that he has dreamed of, with the assurance that if his partner wants to end things, she will say so. The controllee can allow things to continue just a moment or two longer than she might otherwise, knowing that everything will cease the moment she wants it to. A safe word can be like the sleeping pill you keep next to the bed. You sleep very well knowing you can take it if you need to.

Now that we understand the rules of the game, the next step is to find out whether your partner might be interested in sharing your fantasy. Earlier in this book, I discussed the idea of bookmarking. Slip a bookmark into one of the stories in this section (or any other, of course) and let your partner slowly, in private, adjust to something that might be completely new. Maybe you'll find that he or she has had a control fantasy for a long time but has never found a way of sharing that with you. You, on the other hand, were willing to take the risk of revealing that you'd like to play this type of game.

Another way to discover such a desire is in the heat of the moment. Let's say your partner is doing something you particularly enjoy. Say to him, "Don't stop!" Then, when he does stop, as he will at some point, say forcefully, "I didn't tell you that you could stop." You might discover that your partner obediently continues the previous activity. Or your radar might reveal that he or she is suddenly very quiet, or very active, or behaves in a more turned-on way. Take that as a cue that he might enjoy it if you became more dominant from time to time.

Don't discuss it yet; just consider ways to act on what you now know.

Let's begin with a simple form of control.

KATHY AND BILL'S STORY

Bill and Kathy had been spending overnights in Atlantic City for many years, although now that they had three teenaged children, they got away only a few times a year. They particularly enjoyed the poker machines and could spend hours sitting next to each other, betting quarters on the outcome of each new deal. They looked over each other's shoulders as they drew royal flushes and four or five of a kind.

Late one evening, Bill's machine dealt him the ten, jack, king, and ace of spades and a seven of clubs. "This isn't a bad hand," he said, tapping Kathy on the shoulder.

Kathy looked at his screen and grinned. "Not at all," she said as Bill pushed the hold button beneath the four good cards.

"It would be nice, but it's next to impossible."

Although he knew it well, he looked up at the payoff list. "One thousand coins. That's two hundred and fifty dollars."

"Don't count your money yet, love."

"I'm not." His finger poised over the deal button, he said, "I know it's a long shot, but how about a bargain? If this doesn't come in, you are mine to do with what I wish for an hour before we go to bed."

"Okay, and if it does, you have to buy me the best dinner in town with your winnings."

"Done," Bill said, pressing the button. The seven of clubs became the jack of diamonds. "Ah well, at least I have a paying pair."

They played the machines for another hour, had a few good hands, and finally cashed in and walked out, having lost about ten dollars between them for the evening. "Nightcap?" Bill asked.

"Nah. I had three of those delicious Bloody Marys at the machine. I'm a bit tipsy as it is."

Bill pushed the elevator button and said, "You know you owe me an hour of servitude."

"Huh?" Kathy said.

"You mean you've forgotten our bet? The royal flush earlier?"

"Oh, right. I didn't really think you were serious."

"Well, I am." The elevator doors opened, and when they were inside, he pushed the button for the third floor. "You belong to me for an hour, starting when we get to the room." The indicator light flashed 3 and the doors opened. "Think about that. I can make you do anything I want. Or," he said, pausing, "I can do whatever I want to you." As they walked down the hall, he pulled the room key from his pocket and handed it to Kathy. "Open it."

Kathy took the key and opened the door. Bill placed his hand in the small of his wife's back, guided her inside, and closed the door behind them. In the dark, he dropped his jacket on the chair and knelt in front of his wife. He had always loved his wife's legs, and now he slid his hand up the outside, feeling the silkiness of her stockings. "You know," he said, "I've always thought you have the most beautiful legs of anyone in the world. I enjoy touching them, licking them, kissing them, especially when they're covered with your nylon stockings. But I have never gotten my fill. I always have the feeling that you're in a hurry." He slid his hands around the back of Kathy's knees and then slipped his fingers between her nylon-covered thighs.

"I love the way you feel inside of me and I guess I get impatient." She shuddered and her knees buckled.

"I know you do, but I want you just to stand there. You're mine tonight, remember? Now spread your legs; I want to touch them."

Kathy swallowed hard and moved so her feet were about twelve inches apart.

Bill rubbed his fingertips up and down her legs, caressing her calves and knees with his cheek. "God, you feel so good, so sexy." He felt Kathy tremble. Slowly, he stroked, each time getting deeper between his wife's thighs, brushing her nylon-covered pussy lightly. "Do you still keep those little cuticle scissors in your makeup kit?" He got up and flipped on the bathroom light, which left the main room with shafts of light and deep shadow.

"Yes," Kathy said huskily.

"Get them for me."

Kathy found the scissors and gave them to her husband. "Now, back where you were." She stood, legs spread, in front of her husband. "You know," he said, pulling her panty hose down to her thighs, "I love the feel of your legs in stockings."

"That's why I wear them. I love it when you touch me like this."

"But panty hose are the devil's invention. I can stroke your gorgeous thighs, but I can't touch the places I want to touch." He quickly cut Kathy's bikini panties up both sides. "I want to be able to touch your wet pussy." He pulled at the front panel and the destroyed panties were in his hand. He dropped them into the wastebasket. "I wonder what man-hater invented these things." He grabbed the crotch of the panty hose and cut the seam up the center, not quite to the elastic. "That's so much better. You can pull them back up now."

"But baby . . ."

"No *buts*. The bet was for an hour, and we have"—he looked at his watch—"forty-nine more minutes."

Kathy pulled the hose back up over her naked flanks.

"And let's do this without your skirt." He unzipped his wife's miniskirt and tossed it on the chair. As she started to unbutton her blouse, he slapped her hands. "No you don't," he said. "I like you dressed." He chuckled. "Or at least half-dressed."

Bill knelt on the floor at his wife's feet and pressed his cheek against her belly. He kneaded her stocking-covered buttocks, letting his hands roam her hips and thighs. He kissed her pubic bone and listened to her moan. "Want me?"

"Oh yes," Kathy said, grabbing his head and attempting to pull him to his feet. "Let's do it."

"Not so fast. Spread your legs wider."

"But baby . . ."

"Welshing on our bet?"

"No, but . . ."

"Spread 'em."

Kathy widened her stance in her spiked heels until she was almost off balance.

Bill spent the next ten minutes just stroking his wife from the waist down, feeling her tremble with need. "Now," he said, "to see how you taste." He used his thumbs to pull the crotch of the panty hose apart, then stuck his tongue out. From his kneeling position, he could flick the tip of his tongue over his wife's erect clit. "Ummm," he said, "you taste delicious. And you're so wet."

Kathy grabbed a handful of Bill's hair and tried to pull him closer. "Yes baby," she said. "So wonderful. But I can't stand still anymore. My knees won't hold me up. Let's lie down so you can fuck me."

"I want to do it like this," he said, still fully dressed. His tongue worked over her nub until she was screaming with need. "I like it with you standing up." He rubbed her buttocks and hips through her tight nylon hose.

"Please," she begged. "Please."

"Remember our bet. I still have time," Bill said, driving her closer to the edge. "I'm going to make you come standing up, mostly clothed, with just my tongue."

"Oh God," she yelled.

It took only a few moments until Bill felt Kathy arch her back and clamp her thighs around his face. "Yes," she screamed. "Yes! Now! Right now!"

Bill kept licking and sucking until he felt Kathy's

body relax. He sat back on the floor, unzipped his pants, and allowed his hard cock to stand straight up in his lap. "Sit here, baby," he said.

Kathy stared at her husband's cock, caught in a shaft of light from the bathroom. It was bigger than she had ever seen. She straddled his legs and, still dressed from the waist up, sat on his lap, driving his cock inside her through the slit in her panty hose.

Bill felt his cock slip deep into his wife's soaked channel. He cradled her buttocks and raised and lowered her body. Up and down she moved on his body until he felt himself coming. "Don't stop, baby," he yelled. "Don't stop!"

She clenched her vaginal muscles and his semen sprayed into her. He yelled loudly as he came, and together they collapsed on the floor.

A few minutes later, Kathy said, "Wow. That was amazing."

"Yeah, it was," Bill said.

Kathy got up, stripped off her clothes, and climbed into bed. "You know, we have time to play the machines a bit in the morning. And if we bet like this again, we might just have time for a trip back to the room before we go home."

Bill climbed into bed beside his wife. "We just might at that."

This was a very basic, nonthreatening control game, one that anyone can play, since either party can end the game at any time. Kathy didn't have to go along with Bill's requests, but because of their long relationship, mutual trust, and complete understanding, they were able to explore a new area of sexuality.

● ● ●

Patti had her radar up, and her husband, Brad, took a risk. Together, they discovered that they both wanted her to be in control in the bedroom.

PATTI AND BRAD'S STORY

"Have you ever made it in public?" Brad asked.

Nancy blushed and her friend Patti giggled. "I don't believe it," Patti said. "That question actually embarrassed you. I thought you and Joe were unflappable."

"We are," Joe said. "But we have a checkered past. When we were young and foolish, we did some things that we can't believe we actually did."

"But at the time," Joe's wife, Nancy, said, "it seemed like a good idea."

The two couples, Joe and Nancy and Brad and Patti, had been drinking assorted microbrewed beers all evening and the talk had gotten increasingly blunt. "Like what?" Patti pressed. "Come on, tell all."

"No way!" Nancy said.

"But honey," Joe argued, "these guys are our best friends and we should have no secrets."

"Now wait," Brad said. "You don't have to tell us, but after that blush and the pregnant pause, you must know we're dying of curiosity."

"Nancy?" Joe said, squeezing his wife's hand. They sat on twin sofas in the deserted lobby of the small resort in the mountains.

"I guess," Nancy said, "but you tell."

Joe took a drink, then cleared his throat. "It must have been fifteen years ago. It was a costume party, and Nancy dressed in a cop uniform and I was her prisoner. We were actually handcuffed together and everything."

Patti sensed her husband's entire body tense, and he gripped her hand so tightly that it actually hurt. Curious about what had elicited this reaction, she decided to ask him about it later. "And . . ." Patti said.

"Well," Joe continued, "we took a lot of ribbing. One of the *Dirty Harry* movies had been on TV then and people kept kidding us with that line. You know, 'Come on, make my day.' Anyway, since we were handcuffed, someone dared Nancy to make me do sexy things to her right there in public."

Again, Patti felt Brad shudder.

Nancy sighed, then picked up the story. "Well, I drank a lot in those days, so I pulled off my panties, hiked up my skirt, and sat down on the sofa. I spread my knees and made Joe eat me out, right there in this couple's living room."

"God," Joe said, "as I remember it, we were both so hot that you actually came with everyone looking." He looked at Brad and Patti. "Then I pulled her into the bathroom, locked the door, and fucked her brains out."

"Holy cow," Patti said. "That's amazing. I would never have guessed. You don't strike me as the type."

"Actually, it was those handcuffs," Joe said. "Nancy sprung them on me as we walked out of our apartment. She just snapped them on my wrist. Made me so hot . . ."

"Me, too." Nancy blushed again.

"Honey," Brad said suddenly. "If you don't mind, it's really late. Let's call it a night."

"Are you okay?" Patti asked.

"Actually, I've got a bit of a headache."

Oh damn, Patti thought, there goes any fun in bed later. Not tonight—he has a headache. They stood up and the two couples separated and retired to their individual cabins.

When Patti and Brad had closed the door behind them, Brad stretched out on the bed, looking decidedly uncomfortable. "What's the matter, darling?" Patti said. "Something you ate maybe?"

"Yeah, that must be it."

"Or maybe you're tense. While Nancy and Joe were telling that story, I thought you were going to break my knuckles. Did you find the story that shocking?"

"No. It's nothing."

Patti looked at her husband of sixteen years. A second marriage for each of them, with five children between them, it was particularly delightful that they had gotten to spend this weekend away with Nancy and Joe. Patti sat on the edge of the bed and touched Joe's forehead. "You don't feel warm. But I know you very well, and something's wrong."

When Brad remained silent, Patti wheedled, "Baby, tell me. It isn't a headache, is it? It's that conversation. Was it that story they told?" His pointed silence made her continue. "The fact that they made it in public? Does that make you think less of them?"

"Don't be silly. Of course not."

"Then what?"

Brad appeared to be struggling, searching for the right words. "It was . . . well . . . the idea of her having him in handcuffs that bothered me."

"It shouldn't upset you. Some people enjoy that power stuff." She thought about her first husband. "Actually, Nick and I used to play that way occasionally."

Brad was astonished. "You did?"

"Just a few times. He tied me up once, but I didn't like not being in control. I enjoyed the few evenings when I tied him up." When she saw the amazed expression on Brad's face, she quickly added, "I'm sorry. I didn't mean to bring up old lovers."

"That's okay," Brad said. "I just never suspected that you could be into that."

"Are you?"

"Never. At least not in real life. It's too kinky."

"I don't think it's kinky at all. I tried it and it was fun. Anyway, who's to decide what's kinky and what's just kicky?" When Brad said nothing, Patti continued. "I enjoyed being in control and having Nick at my mercy."

Brad shuddered, then said in almost a whisper, "I used to have fantasies in which I was tied up and teased."

"Oh," Patti whispered.

"I'm sorry. I didn't mean anything. Fantasies are just fantasies, and you don't—"

Patti interrupted. "You said 'used to.' Do you still fantasize about being tied up?"

"It's just a fantasy. Not anything I'd really like to do."

"No?" Patti quickly pulled Brad's arms down to his sides and straddled his hips, trapping his forearms against his hips with her knees. "Not even a little bit?" Brad's gaze was locked on Patti's eyes, but he remained silent. "I asked you a question," Patti said, her voice louder and stronger. "Would you like to be tied up?"

"Yes." His voice was almost inaudible.

"Then what?" Patti watched the battle behind Brad's eyes; then she felt his body relax.

"I'd like you to tie me up, if you think it would give you pleasure."

A grin slowly spread across Patti's face. "It would give me great pleasure." Without hesitation, Patti stretched out on top of Brad's body, and, pulling his arms straight out from his sides, pressed his wrists into the bed. She touched his mouth with hers and felt an unusual amount of excitement and passion in Brad's kiss. The full weight of her body on Brad's, she deepened the kiss until her tongue was dueling with his. She moved, arranging and rearranging her mouth on his while he remained still, returning the kiss but not initiating any movement.

She raised her head and looked into Brad's eyes. "You're mine, for tonight," she said. "Say it."

"I'm yours for tonight."

"And I can do anything."

"Anything," Brad whispered.

"And you won't come unless I allow it."

A tremor ran through Brad's body. "I won't come unless you allow it."

Patti ground her hips into Brad's tremendous hard-on, feeling his pelvis move beneath her. He hadn't been so hungry so fast in years. "Don't move," she ordered.

Patti got up, rummaged through her suitcase, and pulled out a silk scarf she had thought of wearing to dinner one evening. Using a pair of small scissors from her sewing kit, she soon had four long strips of material. Then she looked at Brad, who still had his arms extended from the shoulder. "There are rules," she said, then explained about safe words. When they had agreed on the words *holler uncle,* Patti tied one strip around his right wrist, then tied it to the bed frame. Quickly, she tied the other wrist.

"Now, let's see," she said, gazing at Brad's immobilized arms. "We have to remove your sweatshirt." She took the small scissors and cut up the center. "Lucky we packed a few more of these." When she had cut to the neck, she separated the sides and exposed Brad's hairy chest. "I've always wondered about men's nipples," she said. "In the books, it says that they can be as sensitive as a woman's. I've never found it to be so before, but . . ."

She perched on the edge of the bed and leaned over Brad's body. With the flat of her tongue, she stroked Brad's right nipple. "You know, you taste very good."

Brad was writhing, pulling against the silk strips that held him.

"Is what I'm doing exciting you," Patti asked, "or is it just your predicament?"

"It's being tied like this. It's making me crazy."

"Wonderful." She licked Brad's other nipple, then reached down and stroked his jeans-covered cock. "So hard, baby. What would you like now? To fuck me?"

"Oh yes," Brad said.

"Too bad. I'm not nearly ready yet." Patti removed Brad's shoes and socks, then, not wanting to destroy Brad's jeans, she maneuvered them off. She dangled the two remaining silk strips over Brad's erect cock, occasionally brushing the ends over his hot skin. Each time she did, she watched his member twitch. "Remember these," she said, watching his eyes as they stared at the pieces of material.

"Yes," he whispered.

"They are for your ankles. Spread them wide." When he didn't immediately do as she had asked, she barked, "Now!"

Brad spread his legs.

"You like the feeling of being helpless," Patti said, tying one ankle to the bedpost at the foot of the bed.

"Yes," he whispered again.

"That's so good, baby," she purred as she moved around and tied Brad's other ankle. When she was done, she stood up and let her eyes roam over Brad's powerless body. "I want to see you struggle. I want you to know you can't get away."

Brad wiggled and pulled, unable to move more than a few inches. When his body stilled, she said, "I'm very hot, but not nearly ready for your cock yet. As a matter of fact, I may not let you fuck me at all." She slipped her hands inside her jeans and found her wet clit. "Maybe I'll just please myself and leave you until morning."

"No, baby, please," Brad said.

"I love to hear you beg, you know," Patti said, removing her clothes. She took a deep, shuddering breath. She was hotter than she had admitted to Brad, but his reaction was exactly what she had wanted. "Let's see. Maybe you can get me ready." She climbed onto the bed beside Brad's head and crouched so one breast dangled over his mouth. "Suck."

He raised his head and reached for her nipple. When he could reach it, he sucked it into his hot mouth. As he sucked, Patti stroked his cheeks, feeling the muscles as they sparked electricity from her breast to her hungry pussy. "Not so hard," she snapped when he sucked too excitedly. She shifted so her other nipple hung over his mouth. "Say *please*."

"Please. Let me suck your gorgeous tits."

She let him.

When she was too hot to take much more, she climbed over his body until her slippery pussy rested on the shaft of his cock. "Umm, feels good," she said, rubbing almost catlike against the entire length of his cock. She moved so she could massage her clit with his erection.

When he bucked his hips, trying to get the tip of his cock to penetrate, she let her entire weight rest on his body. "You need to hold still."

"I can't. I'm too hungry."

"Too bad. If you don't hold still, you won't get to fuck me at all. On the other hand, if you're a good boy, I might let you enter."

Patti watched the strain build on Brad's face. She could well imagine how difficult it was to hold still, but somehow, he managed. Sinuously, she rubbed her clit over his cock, finding all the places that felt especially good. She reached between her legs, cradled the end of his cock in her palm, and pressed it harder against herself.

"Baby," Brad moaned.

"Don't come. Don't you dare."

"Almost impossible," Brad said through gritted teeth. "Please."

Patti rubbed until she was as close to climax as she could get, then pushed his cock into her slick passage. Brad arched his back and tried to dictate the rhythm of the fucking, but Patti wouldn't let him. "Mine," she growled, moving at her own pace. "Mine."

It took almost no time for both Patti and Brad to reach the point of no return. "Yes," Patti yelled. "Now. Come for me when I come. Right *now*!"

Patti and Brad climaxed almost simultaneously, their spasms lasting for an unusually long time. Finally, Patti collapsed on Brad's body. Panting, they were silent for quite a while.

Finally, Patti raised her head and looked into Brad's eyes. "I hope that was as good for you as it was for me."

"Oh babe," Brad said. "It was not to be believed."

Patti grinned and picked up her scissors. "Let me cut you loose."

"Wait," Brad said. "Can't you untie me?"

"Okay. Why?"

"I wouldn't want to waste those. Who knows, maybe we'll want to use them again."

Patti's grin was wide and her eyes sparkled. "What a clever man you are," she said.

Having children in your married life can be a chore, but it's also a joy. Children are wonderful, and I love mine dearly. I did, however, especially enjoy it when they grew old enough to want to move out. Having a private life again can be a delight, as we'll see in the next chapter.

AGELESS FANTASIES

Here are two more stories for you to enjoy. You will note that in the following story, Ted does not dream of a monogamous activity. People do fantasize about making love to partners other than their husbands or wives. I've had my dreams about George Clooney or Cal Ripkin, Jr. I've even thought about what it might be like to make love to the sexy plumber who arrived at my house to repair a leak. Admit it, you've had them, too.

That doesn't mean, however, that you or I would ever do anything about it. These are fantasies, fun to think about and enjoyable to bookmark.

TED'S FANTASY

Ted had seen her around the office several times during the week. It was hard to miss her. Tall and lithe, about five nine, he guessed, and about 130 pounds, with long, wavy red hair and full round breasts, the kind of woman who got noticed again and again. He found it increasingly difficult to concentrate on his work, knowing she was somewhere in the office.

The day before, he had found out that she was Bonnie Richardson, the new director of Public Relations. Among other things, she was taking over PR for the account that he was working on.

He also found out that she was recently divorced and new to the city, having just moved here to take the job less than a month ago. Thinking about her often started a parade of fantasies running through Ted's mind that he didn't even try to stop.

Ted had just hung up the phone and was gazing out the window of his office, his back to the door, his thoughts on Bonnie.

He turned his chair back toward the door and saw her standing in the doorway to his office. He looked up slowly, drinking in the sight of her long, luscious legs extending from her short, tight skirt, her breasts straining to escape from the light silk blouse that held them captive.

"Hi," she said, "I'm Bonnie Richardson, the new director of PR. Since we haven't been introduced, I thought I'd stop by and say hello."

"H-h-hello," he managed to stammer. "I'm Ted Reynolds, senior project manager."

"I thought that if you had a moment, we could go over this new product line of yours." Her voice was so rich and smooth, it was almost hypnotic.

"S-s-sure," he said. "Come on in."

She sat down in a chair across from his desk and crossed her legs. As she brushed her hair back off her shoulder, she casually touched her right breast. As he watched, her nipple hardened, coming to attention. Ted felt his penis stiffen in his pants. He hoped she wouldn't notice.

Stretching one long, gorgeous leg to its full length, Bonnie kicked the door closed. Ted could just see the top of her stockings peeking from the bottom of her short skirt. "I hate to be interrupted during business *or* pleasure," she said, a sparkle in her eye.

Seeing her long, perfect leg stretched out like that caused Ted's erection to stiffen even more. Did she do that on purpose? he wondered.

"Perhaps you could show me your big . . . project," she said, just a hint of suggestion in her voice.

"O-of course," Ted replied. He knew he'd have to get up to cross the room. He'd just have to hope that she didn't notice the bulge in his pants.

As he got up, however, Bonnie's eyes went straight for his crotch. She didn't say anything, but he knew she had seen. He felt warm and flushed, but he decided to ignore it, as long as she didn't say anything.

As he walked past her, she reached out and touched his hand. "That looks really uncomfortable," she said, staring at the bulge that was exactly at eye level. "Can I help you with that?"

Ted didn't know what to say. Before he could reply, Bonnie had her hand on his cock, massaging it through his pants.

"Mmm," she purred. "Just what I need." She bent closer and kissed it lightly. Ted's hands automatically went to her head and he began stroking her hair.

Ted looked down and saw Bonnie's right hand inside her blouse, under her bra, stroking her large, luscious breast. She was moaning and rubbing her legs together.

"Go sit down," she said, "and leave everything to me."

Ted sat down, as he was told, unsure of what to do next. He sat there transfixed as he watched Bonnie move slowly and sensuously. First, she unbuttoned her blouse, revealing the sheer lace bra she wore underneath. Her nipples were fully erect and easily visible through the flimsy fabric. Reaching up, she cupped both breasts, squeezing them and pinching her nipples, a look of unbridled ecstasy on her beautiful face.

Running her hands down her body, she reached back and unfastened her skirt, letting it fall to the floor, where she kicked it out of the way.

She was wearing black lace thong panties and thigh-high stockings on her long, firm legs. Ted started rubbing his cock through the fabric of his pants, unable to control himself any longer.

Bonnie turned around slowly, spread her legs a little, and, her back to him, bent over, revealing her tight round ass. Placing a hand beneath her panties, she played with her pussy, rubbing her clit until Ted could almost hear the juices flowing.

With her back still toward him, Bonnie removed her bra and then her panties. With only her stockings remaining, she turned to face him.

Ted had never seen a more beautiful woman in his entire life. Tall, firm, and gorgeous, she put most centerfold models to shame. "Are you enjoying the show?" she asked, teasingly.

"Of course," Ted replied, unsure of what to say.

"Good," she said. "Now sit back and enjoy the rest."

With that, she went over to Ted and sat on his lap. Almost instinctively, he wrapped his lips around her left breast, licking and sucking on the beautiful treat. Moaning in ecstasy, Bonnie started grinding her pussy against Ted's erection, his pants still on.

Leaning back, Bonnie's hand went to Ted's crotch. "Poor uncomfortable baby," Bonnie purred. "Let me help."

With that, she slid off Ted's lap and onto the floor beneath his desk. Slowly, she undid Ted's belt and unzipped his pants, pulling them down around his ankles. Then, with a pair of scissors from his desk, she cut his underwear away with two deft strokes, freeing his throbbing tool.

Bonnie stroked it, slowly at first, then faster. Ted couldn't remember the last time it had been this good. With her free hand, Bonnie tickled Ted's balls, lightly running her fingernails over them while she flicked them with her tongue.

"Suck it," Ted begged. "Please suck it."

With a small giggle, Bonnie obliged. She slid her tongue up along Ted's shaft from his balls to the tip, where she licked the head all around, wetting it with her saliva, then blowing on it. Ted shuddered with pleasure. With her hand wrapped around his cock,

Bonnie engulfed the head in her mouth, bobbing and stroking at the same time. On each downstroke, she swallowed a little bit more of his dick, until she had deep-throated the entire thing. With his cock entirely in her mouth, Bonnie started humming, very gently at first, then more insistently. The vibrations were driving Ted crazy.

Releasing the tension a little, Bonnie moved her head up and down again, letting Ted fuck her throat. She could feel his balls tightening and knew that he was about to come. Faster and faster she moved, getting turned on by the sound of Ted's moans and groans. Suddenly, she felt him explode in her mouth, felt the warm white fluid fly down her throat, felt Ted's hands on her head, involuntarily urging her to take it all.

Ted was spent, but after a few moments, Bonnie announced, "Now it's my turn." With that, she stood up, and lay back on Ted's desk, spreading her legs in front of him. Without any further encouragement, he slid his chair forward until he was between the legs of the red-haired goddess and then began to stroke the inside of her thighs with his tongue. He started about midthigh and worked his way upward, stopping just short of Bonnie's clit. Then he skipped over her pussy entirely, moving to the other side and licking and nibbling his way to the midpoint of the opposite thigh. After several repetitions, Bonnie's gasps and sighs had turned to moans and entreaties.

"Don't tease me," she cried. "Do it. Fuck me with your tongue, baby."

Finally, he lightly touched her pussy lips with his tongue, sending a ripple of pleasure throughout Bonnie's body. Unable to control herself any longer, she grabbed his head and pressed it to her hot, throbbing clit.

"Ooo. Lick it. Suck it. Please," she moaned. Finally accommodating her, Ted drew the length of his tongue over her swollen clit, getting a scream of pleasure out of her.

"Yes," she cried. "Yes, yes, yes, yes . . ."

Faster and faster, his tongue flicked over her clit. She grabbed handfuls of his hair, keeping him just where she wanted him. *"Fuck me!"* she shouted, at which point he inserted a finger into her pussy, which pushed her over the edge. Bucking her hips in time to Ted's finger-fucking, Bonnie came in an explosive orgasm. Ted felt her legs tighten around his head as he kept licking and sucking and fucking. . . .

Ted thought that it was all over. He wasn't sure he'd ever be able to move again. But she stood, turned around, and bent over his desk. Her fingers rubbed her still-swollen clit and she screamed, "Don't make me wait, lover! Fuck me now!"

The sight of the beautiful creature bent over his desk, begging for him, was too much for Ted. In an instant, he was rock-hard again. Moving to her, Ted rubbed the head of his dick against Bonnie's pussy, feeling the warm wetness. Lingering over her clit, he rubbed it with the head of his cock until, taking matters into her own hands, Bonnie grabbed the base of his dick and guided it inside her.

Ted's cock slipped inside as if he had been made for her. He started thrusting, slowly at first, then faster and faster. He reached beneath her and grabbed her breasts as she fondled his balls. Both were moaning and groaning loudly enough for the entire office to hear, but neither cared, being totally wrapped up in their mutual pleasure.

"I'm gonna come!" Ted cried.

"Wait for me!"

"I can't!"

"Wait," Bonnie begged.

Ted did his best to maintain control, but the pressure in his dick and his balls was almost too much. Afraid he'd come before she did, he was thrilled when she cried, "I'm going to come, baby. I'm going to come right *now!*"

With that, Ted felt her pussy muscles contract around his dick, squeezing him. He let go also, shooting his hot come way deep inside of Bonnie's pussy. He buried his cock up to his balls, enjoying the sensation of Bonnie's tight cunt squeezing him. She pushed herself against him, wanting to get every drop. They collapsed into Ted's chair, Bonnie seated on his lap, her back to him, his cock still inside her.

Looking seductively over her shoulder at him, Bonnie said, "I was told you were a big man in this company, but . . ."

"Mr. Reynolds?" the voice said to Ted's back.

"Huh?" Ted was suddenly yanked from his reverie. "I'm sorry. I was thinking about the big project I'm working on." He turned and saw a figure standing in his doorway.

"Hi," the voice said, "I'm Bonnie Richardson."

MAGGIE'S FANTASY

"Step to the back. Come on, folks, move back."

Maggie shifted her weight from one soaked foot to the other, trying to make her way to the rear of the crowded bus. As she wiggled her hips past an over-

weight man in a three-piece suit with sour body odor,
she glanced out the bus window. "Shit," she muttered.
"Only Sixty-eighth Street." She found a small space and
clasped the overhead bar in a death grip. With her free
hand, she hiked the strap of her handbag higher on
her shoulder, maneuvered her umbrella so it was held
against the side of her raincoat, and set her briefcase
down close to her calf. Then she took a deep breath
and carefully tucked her purse under her arm to keep
greedy fingers from helping themselves.

Maggie was a forty-six-year-old accountant in a
small firm. She was only about five foot one, with
short mousy brown hair and contact lenses. Her thighs
were larger than she would have liked and her breasts
were smaller. Fortunately, she knew that Frank, her
husband of seventeen years, liked her just as she was.
Her children just thought of her as Mom.

I hate rain in the winter, she thought. The whole
city smells of wet wool, wet hair, and wet shoes. . . .
She shifted her weight again, hearing her feet squoosh
in her soggy low-heeled black pumps.

As the bus lurched forward through the heavy rush-
hour traffic, Maggie looked down at the lucky people
who had seats. She noticed a seated young man who
was calmly reading his newspaper.

YOUTH DEAD IN GANG-RELATED SHOOTING.

FIRE DESTROYS HUNDRED-YEAR-OLD LANDMARK BUILDING.
The man turned the page.

LOWEST FARES IN YEARS TO CARIBBEAN.

Maggie sighed. The Caribbean. She and Frank had
traveled to Saint Martin on their honeymoon and
had promised themselves they would return someday. Oh how she wished she were there with him
right now.

Maggie let her gaze wander to the rivers of water running down the bus window. Reality slipped away.

She was walking along the beach, the sand wet and hard beneath her bare feet, the warm sun beating down on her bare shoulders. She squinted in the bright sunlight and saw that a few soft white clouds dotted the high azure sky. A large wave broke and she felt the spray dampening her skin and the tiny black bikini she wore.

She reached up to brush a lock of long chestnut brown hair away from her face and ran her fingers through its soft waves. She loved to wear it loose like this, letting it fall in long, deep waves down to her waist. As she walked, she felt it sway against the skin on her back.

She glanced down. Her figure was perfect. High, full breasts and a flat stomach, long, shapely legs and slender thighs, all fully revealed in her tiny bikini. And she was beautiful. Her eyes were the blue of deep, peaceful water and were fringed by long dark lashes. Her skin was clear and youthful.

She looked to her right and smiled at Frank, dressed in a tiny kelly green bathing suit, his body young and so tight and sexy. Maggie looked at his shoulders, broad and deeply tanned; his belly flat, with cords of well-developed muscles; his strong thighs and bare feet.

"Your nose is getting a little red," Frank said. "Maybe we'd better get out of the sun."

Maggie reached up and touched her nose. It was a little tight and tender. "I suppose we should."

"How about over there?" Frank asked, pointing to a small wooden platform surrounded by six vertical wooden poles, which, in turn, supported a roof of palm fronds.

"Okay," she said, dipping her toes in the cool water one last time. Then, hand in hand, the couple ran quickly across the hot white sand and jumped onto the shaded platform, grateful for the cool feeling of the boards beneath their overheated feet. "It's amazing how hot that sand gets," Maggie said. She looked around for someplace to sit.

"I'll get something. Stay here." Frank darted away, grabbed an extrawide plastic-webbed lounge chair from the beach, and set it up on the platform. "Rest here while I get us one of those delightfully sinful banana daiquiris from the beach bar." He planted a quick kiss on the tip of her nose and started down the beach. "I'll be right back," he called over his shoulder.

As Frank walked away, Maggie watched his tight ass move beneath the bright green spandex. She watched the play of the muscles of his back and shoulders. As he broke into a run, she smiled at the beautiful proportions of his body as it moved.

Maggie dusted the sand from her feet, stretched out in the lounge chair, and closed her eyes. A few minutes later, Frank returned with two frosty glasses filled with thick white liquid and crushed ice.

"You look very sexy stretched out like that," Frank said as he settled on the foot of the chair and handed Maggie her drink. "Very sexy indeed." Silently, they sipped their drinks and watched the waves.

"Delicious," Maggie said, setting her glass on the floor next to her chair.

"Almost as delicious as you," her husband said. Frank lifted one of Maggie's feet and kissed the tender area under her arch. Then he slid the tip of his tongue from her heel to the base of her big toe. "Very tasty indeed," he added.

Maggie pulled her foot back and giggled. "That tickles, honey."

Frank grabbed her foot, leaned over, and bit the end of her big toe. "I bet that doesn't."

"Ow, you brute."

Again, Frank bit her toe, then licked the end and sucked it into his mouth. His tongue swirled over the end of Maggie's toe, both tickling and arousing her.

"Nice." She sighed.

Frank set his glass down beside Maggie's, shifted around on the chair, and pressed the ball of his thumb into the arch of Maggie's foot. He alternately massaged her foot and sucked her big toe.

"Umm," Maggie purred. "That feels wonderful."

Frank placed his hands on either side of Maggie's calf and began to massage her leg. He dug his fingers deeply into her calf, then stroked her shin with featherlight touches. He then ran the nail of his index finger across the back of Maggie's knee.

"That's a very sexy spot," Maggie said, suddenly breathless. "Maybe we'd better go back to the hotel. You know, take a nap . . . or whatever."

"I want to 'whatever' right here," Frank said, still holding his wife's knee and tickling the back of it.

"Not right here," Maggie protested. "Anyone can see us. It's too public."

"Look around," Frank said. "We're in the deep shade and the sun is too bright for anyone to be able to see us. Anyway, there's no one around."

"You can't be serious," Maggie protested, not too loudly, though. "I mean . . . "

Frank slid his hands up Maggie's leg, softly stroking

the flesh on the inside of her thigh. He leaned over and flicked his tongue across her inner thigh. "You taste just a bit salty." He picked up his glass, now dripping with condensed moisture, and ran it up the inside of Maggie's leg. Before she could squeal, he licked up the wet trail with his warm tongue. "Oh baby, let me love you," he murmured.

Maggie looked around and saw no one. As Frank continued to caress her, Maggie knew that if they didn't stop now, they would be unable to stop later. She quickly admitted to herself that she didn't want him to stop. "You feel so good," she whispered, giving him consent to continue.

Frank slid up Maggie's body until he was lying beside her on the wide chair. He placed one hand on either side of her face and kissed her lower lip. She kept her lips relaxed as he kissed and nibbled first her lower lip, then her upper. Then he pressed his mouth fully against hers and pushed his tongue against her lips. She opened her mouth and let his tongue slowly explore the inside of her mouth.

As Maggie moved to press her tongue into Frank's mouth, he pulled back. "Just lie there and do nothing. Let me make love to you in my own way."

Maggie sighed and smiled. She would let him do anything he wanted.

She felt Frank slide his hands around her neck and untie the top of her bathing suit. He sat back and pulled the tiny scraps of fabric down so that her full breasts spilled out. He quickly unfastened the lower strap and dropped the cloth onto the platform.

Maggie let her eyes close and head drop back as Frank cupped her breasts in his hands. "So beautiful," he whispered. "Your breasts are just the right size to fill my hands, and so white and soft." He used his thumbs to caress her nipples until they were tight and puckered. "And your nipples get so hard."

He pulled a heavy lock of her long hair from behind her and held it tightly, making the end into a brush. He dusted the hair across her lips and cheeks, down her neck, and across her chest. Then he flicked the lock of hair across her exposed breasts. "So beautiful," he whispered.

When Maggie opened her eyes and tried to sit up, Frank said, "Just lie there, close your eyes, and let me pleasure you." Maggie sighed, lay back, and closed her eyes.

Frank bent down, picked up his drink, and held it over his wife's body. Soon, a drop of cold water trickled down the outside of the glass and dropped on her breast. He used the brush of hair to paint her flesh. Frank let the water fall drop by drop on his wife's heated skin, then brushed it with her hair.

He let the hair fall so that it covered her right breast, with only her enlarged nipple poking through. He took a large mouthful of the banana-flavored liquid in his glass, then quickly bent over. Without swallowing, he drew her tight left nipple into his mouth, letting the cold daiquiri dribble onto her skin.

"That's cold," Maggie protested, twisting away.

Frank placed his palm flat against the cold skin. "Not for long. I'll warm it." He massaged her breast with his rough palm. "Hot now, baby?"

"Oh God," Maggie said.

Frank took another mouthful of banana daiquiri, pushed her hair aside, and sucked Maggie's other nipple into his cold mouth. As he felt her move, he drew his mouth away and placed his palm against her flesh.

He swirled his finger around her breast, ending with all five fingers squeezing her nipple.

He swallowed his drink and held Maggie's glass so that she could have a swallow, as well. Then Frank kissed along his wife's rib cage and down her belly. He pressed the tip of his tongue into her belly button, pulling back and pressing as though his tongue were fucking her navel.

Maggie was awash in sensation. She reached out and tangled her fingers in her husband's long dark hair, pulling him more tightly against her.

"Feels good, baby?" he asked.

"You feel so good."

"Then take this off," he moaned, pulling at the bottom of Maggie's bikini. Quickly, she raised her hips and slid it off.

Frank slid his hands under Maggie's bottom, lifted her hips off the chair, and threw her legs over his shoulders. He licked the length of her slit with the flat of his tongue. "So slippery," he said. "So wet for me. You're hot for me, aren't you, baby?"

"Oh yes."

Frank flicked the tip of his tongue across her clit, then sucked and drew the swollen button into his mouth. Maggie's fingers, still entangled in his hair, pulled him more tightly against her. "Such a hungry girl," he purred. Then he pressed his pointed tongue against her opening and pushed it into her. He pulled out, then pressed inside again, now fucking her with his tongue.

"You're going to make me come if you keep doing that," Maggie cried.

"Not yet," Frank said, standing up quickly and pulling off his bathing suit. "Open your eyes and see what you do to me."

Maggie opened her eyes and stared at her husband's cock. She'd never seen him so aroused. "Show me," she whispered. "Show me how hard you are."

Frank wrapped one hand around his cock and squeezed, watching a drop of liquid form at the tip of his penis. It was now taking all his self-control not to jump on Maggie's body and fuck her until he came. Not yet, he told himself. Make it last.

Maggie reached down and picked up her drink. She filled her mouth with the icy liquid and motioned for Frank to come closer. He knew what she was going to do and he walked near the head of the chair.

She grasped his cock and slid it into her mouth. She realized that the combination of the cold liquid and her warm tongue might make Frank come in her mouth, but she didn't care. As Maggie slid her hands around to cup his buns, she felt him clenching his ass, trying not to climax.

Frank pulled his cock from Maggie's warm mouth and she swallowed her drink. They had both held out as long as they could, but now they could wait no longer.

Frank knelt between Maggie's legs, lifted her hips, and drove his rigid cock deep into her steaming body. He used one thumb to rub her clit as he pumped his hips.

Maggie reached around and grabbed his buttocks tightly with both hands. She pulled him closer, then pulled her body back. "You pleasured me; now let me fuck you," she said, exciting him with her language as well as with her body. "Open your eyes and watch me while I give you joy."

Frank opened his eyes and watched Maggie's breasts bounce as she loved him, using her body to fuck him. "Oh yes. Come on, baby," he cried, watching the ecstasy on her face. "Take it all. Fuck me with your hot pussy."

His words drove them both over the edge. "Don't stop," she cried as they both climaxed. "Not yet." She came for what seemed like long minutes, using her hands and body to control Frank's long thrusts.

"Yes, more, baby." Frank pounded, draining every drop in his body.

Finally, Maggie held him tightly against her as they both collapsed onto the chair. Breathing heavily, she opened her eyes. As she glanced toward the waterline, she saw a young couple watching them. The man smiled and enfolded the woman in his arms. They kissed, then resumed their walk down the beach.

"That was sensational," Frank said.

"Umm," Maggie purred.

"Getting off, lady," the man in the three-piece suit snapped impatiently, bringing Maggie back to the present. She bent down and peered out the fogged-over bus window. "Oh damn," she muttered. "I almost missed my stop." Maggie shifted her pocketbook and umbrella, picked up her briefcase, and hustled off the bus.

She opened her umbrella, but not quickly enough to keep a cold dribble from trickling down the back of her neck. "Shit," she said as she trudged toward her apartment building.

As she entered the building's foyer, she almost crashed into her husband. "Oh, poor baby," he said. "Look at you. You look drowned."

"You're drenched, too," Maggie said, looking over her bedraggled husband. She smiled at him. "I love you, you know."

He smiled. "I know. Me, too." Frank walked toward the elevator, breaking the momentary spell.

"This rain is too much," Maggie said, pressing the elevator button. "What a day. And the weatherman says it might change to snow this evening." She spotted a brown paper bag in Frank's arm. "What've you got there?" she asked.

Frank smiled and sighed. "For some reason, I was thinking about Saint Martin today." The elevator door slid open and they stepped inside. "Remember our honeymoon?" Frank reached around his wife and pressed the button for the fifth floor. His arm trapped his wife in the corner of the elevator and he placed a long, leisurely kiss on her wet mouth. "Umm," he purred. "Anyway, I was thinking about those banana daiquiris we had. The kids are both out for the evening, so I stopped and got some cans of daiquiri mix, a few ripe bananas, and a bottle of rum. I thought this might be a wonderful evening to relax together, just you, me, and a blender."

"Sounds like a terrific idea," Maggie said, smiling. "Just great."

4

The Empty Nest

One evening, a priest, a minister, and a rabbi were sitting around arguing.

"Life begins at conception," the priest said. "When the sperm and egg unite, you have an embryo, and an embryo is life."

"Not at all," the minister replied. "Life begins at birth, when the blood courses through the veins and the lungs begin to take in air."

For many minutes, the two men argued. "Conception." "Birth." "Conception." "Birth." Finally, the two men turned to the silent rabbi. "Give us your opinion, Rabbi. When does life begin?"

"Well," the older man said after a long pause, "when the kids go to college and the dog dies, that's when life begins."

Isn't that the truth? In the spring of the year during which my elder daughter was to leave for college, Baron von Hound, our one-hundred-plus-pound German shepherd, died. Although all of us were sad to end our eight-year relationship with Baron, he was distinctly anti-social and had curtailed many of our family plans. Once

Baron was gone and my daughters were away at school, life became much simpler. I loved my empty nest.

In the past, before she had a life outside the kitchen, a woman had a difficult time carving out a job for herself once the children were gone. Most women were full-time wives and mothers and were untrained for any work outside the home. Once the children were gone, she had to resort to bridge clubs and charity work to fill the hours in which she used to cook, clean, nurture, and generally exhaust herself. Her "empty nest" was a lonely place, which she worked hard to fill.

Today, things are different. Most women have had full- or part-time jobs outside the home for a long time, and now that the little ones are out and gone, her empty nest has finally given her and her husband the opportunity and free time to explore all types of new experiences. You and your partner now have space, time, energy, and, most important, privacy.

Despite all the newfound freedom and all the articles about spicing up your love life, there are sexual problems for the empty nesters, too. The most basic problem for our generation is the collection of long-held and often erroneous ideas that revolve around sex. Like me, those in their forties and fifties were brought up in a communication wasteland. I had a very enlightened mother who answered all my questions and helped me understand the mechanics of sex. The emotional side, however, was left pretty much undiscussed.

When I married, I thought that a woman was a vessel who should always be ready to receive her husband's lovemaking. It was my sexual "job description," so to speak. Talk about what *I* wanted? Of course not.

It's not that I suppressed my urge to discuss matters; it's that the urge never existed. And be the instigator of lovemaking? Not a chance. That was the man's job, poor soul. He always had to make the first move, and, of course, risk the rejection that went with it. That was the way it was between my husband and me, and, unfortunately, I don't think we were unusual.

How my marriage would have continued, I don't know. After seventeen years, my husband and I separated and I entered the sexual revolution with my entire being. Would I have discovered the pleasures of adventurous sex otherwise? Would I have talked to my husband about my desires and needs? I can't be sure. But, as I think back today, with almost twenty years of hindsight, I tend to think not. To the best of my recollection, we had developed such deeply ingrained habits that they would have been hard to discover, much less break. Was I unhappy sexually? Sometimes. Did I have any idea how to fix the situation? Not a clue.

Nowadays, of course, every TV talk show, every women's magazine, and every conversation in the nail salon all seem to revolve around a woman's needs and desires, sexual or otherwise. Would that have changed me, or would I have evolved? I can't say. Have you evolved?

Now is the time for women my age to crack that mold and become the aggressors occasionally. Yes, it's difficult. Just the act of lighting candles on the dresser can feel silly or awkward. But there are many subtle ways to start becoming more aggressive. Shop for sexy lingerie, buy and wear an exotic perfume, have a special bottle of wine chilled when he gets home from work, or plan a romantic weekend getaway. Tell him in various ways, both overt and covert, that you're interested in a playful evening together.

Well, it's time. If not now, when?

Men, you have some old baggage to deal with, as well. I have the feeling that you have fantasies you might play out with a stranger, if it weren't entirely too dangerous. But with your wife, your partner? Not her. She's not that kind of woman. That's another of those stereotypical ideas that should have disappeared with the end of the 1950s but, unfortunately, is so ingrained that you don't even realize you believe it.

There's another problem with a long relationship. You know each other's sexual buttons much too well. You've fallen into sexual habits—you cuddle in a particular position in bed, touch in that special place that says, Wanna? and your partner wiggles in that special way that says, Okay. You advance through the same moves to the same caresses and end in the same position. Bad? No. Predictable and maybe a bit boring? Yes. A sexual technique that drove a man or woman crazy when first tried cools and becomes commonplace with repeated use. And an idea that wasn't wonderful when first tried might be just the thing with the passage of time and some newfound privacy.

What's more, for many people who've seen each other's naked bodies 365 nights a year for twenty years, those bodies aren't automatically a sexy turn-on any more.

So here you two are, with time, space, energy, and privacy. How can you turn up the volume on your sex life? Begin by trying to shed those old habits and outmoded ideas. Are those traditions difficult to discover and get rid of? Of course. But there is so much fun out there to have, it's a shame if a few cobwebs keep you from delightful pleasures.

Like what? Now you have an empty house. You can arrive home from a party, tear each other's clothes off, and make love on the living room floor; or you might turn the third bedroom into a playroom with a king-sized bed, lots of pillows, and a collection of toys. You can do anything you want—anything.

Let's start with Betty. She and her husband had shared a fantasy for a long time, but only now did she work up the courage to act it out.

BETTY AND TOM'S STORY

Betty looked down at the bed, spread with a large white towel, and almost chickened out. I want to do this, she said to herself. I want to play out this fantasy we both have, but I don't know whether I'll do it right. I don't know whether I can make him as hot as he was the night we first talked about this. She remembered that evening. Tom had a doctor's appointment the following morning and he had confessed his long-standing fantasy about being "examined" by a female. "I'm glad I've never had a woman doctor," he had said. "I would have such a hard-on that I'd probably totally embarrass myself and her."

Well, Betty thought as she arranged a few props on the bedside table, I hope this works out.

"Honey, I'm home." The front door slammed. Betty had selected an evening when Tom had already had dinner and an after-dinner appointment.

"I'll be out in a minute," Betty called. She took a deep breath and walked down the short hall to the living room. "The doctor is ready for you, sir," she said, her voice small and shaky.

Tom looked at his wife, who was dressed in a white uniform top and pants and white shoes, her short gray hair tucked under a little white cap. "Why are you dressed like that?" he asked.

Betty took another deep breath. Come on, baby, she silently urged Tom, play along. We've done this kind of thing before. "I said the doctor will see you now."

She watched his eyes travel over her outfit and saw comprehension dawn. "Oh," he said, clearing his throat. "I forgot I had an appointment today."

Damn, I love you, she thought. "Well, you're right on time. If you'll take off all your clothes and leave them in the bathroom, we're ready for you in here." She pointed toward the bedroom door.

"All my clothes?" Tom stared, and Betty could see the mounting excitement in his eyes. But, she realized, there was a bit of fear there, too.

Plunging ahead, Betty said, "You can leave your shorts on for now and come in when you're ready. The doctor will be waiting for you." She reentered the bedroom, giving Tom time to adjust and to decide whether to play out this fantasy or end it. Trust me, baby. Let's play this. She didn't have long to wait.

Stripped to his shorts, Tom opened the bedroom door. "Oh my Lord," he said. Betty had turned on all the lights, so the room was extremely bright. It smelled of disinfectant and alcohol.

Betty saw the unease written all over Tom's face. She knew what it was like to be suddenly faced with a fantasy like this, because he had helped her act out a few of hers over their long years together. And she trusted him to let her know if she was carrying things too far. But for now, he needed a little push. "Come on, sir, I'm waiting, and I have other patients after you."

She watched Tom square his shoulders and walk toward the bed. "What should I do?" he said in a shy voice.

"Lie down here," Betty said, pointing to the towel-covered area of the bed. "On your back."

Tom complied. "This feels sort of silly," he said, slipping out of the fantasy.

"But hot?" Betty asked.

Tom looked into his wife's eyes. "Yes," he whispered. "Very hot."

Slipping back into her professional voice, she said, "I understand you've been having some abdominal pain."

"That's right," Tom said, back in character.

Betty took a pair of latex gloves from the bedside table and pushed her hands inside very slowly. One finger at a time, she smoothed the white plastic over her fingers while Tom watched every move. She pressed on his abdomen above the waistband of his shorts. "Here?"

"Yes," he said.

"Lower?"

"Yes. There, too."

Working around Tom's now very large erection, Betty pressed on various areas of his belly. "Very puzzling."

"Is it?"

"I don't quite understand what could be the source of your pain." She slipped her gloved hand under Tom's shorts and grasped his hard cock. When he gasped, she smiled. "It could be this, I guess," she said, squeezing. She took his balls in her other hand. "And these, too." She squeezed with both hands.

"Oh God, baby." Tom's breathing was ragged and his entire body trembled.

Betty withdrew her hands. "But maybe not. I need to learn more about your condition." She paused. "Turn over. I need to check for internal problems."

"What?" Tom stared at her.

"I said, turn over. And remove your shorts, too."

"Babe . . ."

She knew she was close to something they had alluded to but had never actually done, and she needed to be sure that Tom understood and agreed. "You know what type of exam I need to do."

Betty watched Tom obviously weighing what was happening. Then he stood up, pulled off his shorts, and stretched out on the towel. Betty ran her gloved hands over Tom's back, pressing and kneading. "Any of that hurt?"

"No . . ." He paused, then added, "No, Doctor."

Betty let out a pent-up breath. "That's good. I'll be just a moment." Betty took a long, slim, flanged dildo from the drawer of the bedside table. "I really need to check you thoroughly."

Tom stared at the dildo. "Where did you get *that*?"

"It's a standard instrument," Betty responded, "for the kind of exam you need right now."

Tom's breathing was rapid and uneven. "Oh."

"I'll be ready in just a moment." Tom's eyes never left her hand as Betty slowly covered the dildo with lubricant. She looked down and watched as Tom squirmed, rubbing his erection against the towel. "You must hold still, sir, so I can complete my exam."

She smiled as she watched Tom's attempts to control his body. "I must make this probe very slippery, you know," she said, trying for a conversational tone. "This procedure isn't very painful, but I must slip this instrument deep inside." She knew her description was adding to Tom's excitement. "Now I'll just lubricate your anal area, too." She took a finger full of gel and used the other hand to part Tom's cheeks. "Nice and slippery." She touched the cold gel to Tom's ass and watched him jump. She knew the combination of sensations must be driving him higher. She pushed the tip of her finger against his anal sphincter. "This won't hurt a bit." She pressed but didn't penetrate. For a few moments, she rubbed the area around Tom's puckered anus and felt his effort to hold still.

"Will you be much longer?" Tom asked with a groan.

"No, sir. I'm ready now."

She spread his cheeks wider, then touched his anus with the tip of the dildo and pushed. The slender column of plastic easily slipped inside. She pushed gently and watched it sink into his body until the wide flange rested against his cheeks. "Now see? That wasn't so bad, was it?"

Tom merely grunted.

"Good. I just need to check out one more thing. Raise up on your knees slightly." Betty knew her husband well, and it was obvious to her that he was losing control. She grinned and repeated her instruction.

As he pulled his knees beneath his belly and pushed his ass into the air, Betty squeezed a large puddle of lubricant into the palm of one hand, then held the flange of the dildo in place with the other. When she could reach between his legs, she slid her slippery hand over Tom's balls and grasped his cock. Pumping with one hand and sliding the dildo in and out with the other, it was only a moment before Tom came, shooting semen onto the towel beneath him. Betty pumped and pumped until Tom's cock was drained, then pulled out the dildo, removed the towel, and pushed him gently onto his back.

Still fully dressed in her doctor's outfit, Betty stretched out on the bed beside Tom and put her head on his shoulder. "I didn't go too far, did I?"

"Oh baby, no. That was so hot. You did great."

"Thanks," she said in a small voice. "Maybe you might want to do something like that to me sometime."

"You mean that you might like . . ."

"Just think about it."

"What I'm already thinking," said Tom, "is that you're long overdue for your next complete physical exam. And I know the best doctor in town."

Betty was really brave to take the chances she did, but she got quite a reward. And your fantasy playing can be as simple as making love with the lights on or lighting candles. It could be giving your partner a long hand massage or beginning by brushing her hair. It certainly doesn't have to involve something as risky as anal sex.

A warning: If you decide to try anal penetration, as Betty did, there are a few precautions.

First, select a dildo with a wide flange on the end. Because the vaginal passage is of finite length and closed at the internal end, dildos for vaginal penetration can be retrieved with ease if they disappear into that body cavity. The anal opening leads directly to the intestinal tract and therefore has no internal closure. Nothing should be inserted far enough to get lost.

Second, the anal passageway isn't naturally lubricated the way the vaginal one is. Therefore, to prevent damage, a lot of lubricant is necessary. One very sexy way to lubricate an anal dildo is to slip a prelubricated condom over the plastic.

Third, if you decide to try penile penetration of the anus, condoms are mandatory. We all know about the danger of disease transmission during anal intercourse. If you want to try this off-center but, to many, thoroughly enjoyable lovemaking technique, two well-lubricated condoms should be worn and carefully removed before any vaginal penetration.

Fourth, don't touch any vaginal tissues with anything that has been in contact with the anus. There are bacteria that live in the digestive system, and, if they find a warm home in the vagina, they can give you serious infections.

TRY SOMETHING NEW:
TOYS

Now that the kids are no longer snooping in your room, it might be time to develop a toy collection. I have a red quilted bag that sits beside Ed's bed and contains a varied assortment of sex toys. Ed was the brave one who purchased my first dildo—yes, I was over forty before I ever owned a sex toy—and I still have the vibrator that Ed and I purchased from a specialty store in Manhattan more than ten years ago.

In the story that follows, Alice did a bit of shopping and surprised her husband, Mario, at a business dinner. But Mario managed to turn the tables, and a wonderful night of bliss ensued.

ALICE AND MARIO'S STORY

"I'm really sorry that I had to drag you to this thing," Mario said to his wife as they rang his boss's doorbell.

"Honey," Alice said, a strange gleam in her eye, "not to worry. You may find you actually enjoy this evening."

Mario shrugged. "If I do, it will be the first time. John Harper and that wife of his give me a pain in the—Good evening, Mrs. Harper," he said to the over-jeweled, overdressed, and overly made-up woman who opened the door.

"You must remember to call me Roberta, Mario dear," the woman said, extending a bejeweled hand for him to touch. "I'm so glad you could make it."

"I wouldn't have missed this dinner for anything," Mario said, squeezing his wife's hand in an effort not to laugh or gag. "And Roberta, you remember Alice."

"Yes, of course. Come in."

Mario put his coat and his wife's jacket in an upstairs bedroom, then joined his wife in the living room. As a jacketed waiter passed, he grabbed a flute of champagne for Alice and one for himself. "Lord," he said, sotto voce as he handed the glass to his wife. He looked around at all the business types who filled the room. "It looks like this evening is going to be longer than most." He spent a few minutes pointing out three of the firm's newest clients and their wives. "I guess I have to go and be nice to the folks with the money."

Alice leaned close to her husband's ear. "I just want you to know something before you mingle. I'm not wearing any panties." Mario's startled expression told

Alice that she had achieved just the effect she had intended.

For a while, Alice had realized that their love life needed a bit of spice. They had had a delightfully creative sex life when they were first married, but over time it had become predictable. A few weeks earlier, she had gotten a wonderfully outrageous idea from a women's magazine. Then at a neighborhood erotic toy store, she had added her own imaginative twist. That afternoon, she had decided that this was just the evening to try it. And Mario would be able to do nothing about it.

"You're what?" he said through his teeth, trying not to yell.

"I'm not wearing any underwear. And later . . ." Alice moved away and quickly involved herself in a conversation with Roberta and a startlingly beautiful woman from Georgia. Out of the corner of her eye, Alice watched Mario get snagged into a discussion of the firm's latest project. A little while later, Mario stood alone. "Mario, you seem preoccupied," his boss said, draping his arm around Mario's shoulder. "You don't seem to be entirely with it this evening," he continued, loudly enough for Alice to overhear. "Is anything wrong?"

"No, no," Mario said, glancing at Alice. "Not at all."

"That's good to hear," Mr. Harper said. "Now go and do your thing." The older man almost pushed Mario toward two of the new clients.

Fifteen minutes later, Mario seemed to have forgotten Alice's earlier statement, so she walked up behind him and whispered in his ear, "And I'm wearing that garter belt and stockings you like so much. You know, I can feel the silk of my slip against my bare ass." Again she walked away.

"Dinner is ready," Roberta said.

Throughout the first course, Mario cast glances at his wife down the length of the long table, but by the time dessert was served, Mario was engaged in an animated conversation with one of the other women. Alice rose and excused herself, and by the time she returned from the powder room, the guests were all in the living room, chatting.

Alice spotted Mario on the sofa, crossed the room, and settled beside him. "I put my panties back on," she said softly, "to hold the dildo inside."

To Mario's stare, Alice added, "You heard me."

"What are you doing to me?" Mario moaned softly, moving to a less constrained position. "Harper will fire me if I screw this up."

"You won't," Alice said. "You're too good at what you do to let that happen. I just want you to know what you have to look forward to later."

"How could I forget?"

"Oh yes, and it vibrates."

"What vibrates?"

"The dildo. I got it last week at the Pleasure Palace Boutique, and it's absolutely silent. It has a remote control, too, and I have it in my purse." She opened her handbag and showed him the small white plastic control unit. "All I have to do is turn it on and . . . well, you can imagine what I'll be feeling."

Mario's knees went weak, but then he smiled. It was either fight or play, and he realized which he wanted to do. Before Alice could stop him, Mario had snatched the control unit from her purse and dropped it into his pocket. "Now I'm in control, darling." He grinned. "Behave or I'll turn this thing on and I'll be able to watch you try to resist the humming in your pussy."

"Hey, wait a minute," Alice said, reaching toward Mario's pocket and trying to retrieve the control unit without making a fuss. "That's not fair."

Mario reached into his pocket and flipped the tiny switch. He could tell by the change in Alice's expression that she felt the vibrator's insistent buzz in her pussy. He flipped the switch off. He grinned. "You know, you're right. It is absolutely silent. No one else will know what I can do by putting my hand in my pocket. But you will." He grinned again. "I wonder what the range of this thing is."

"About fifty feet, it said in the ad." Then she realized what she had said, and she swallowed hard.

"Good. Now go and be a good corporate wife and mingle. But, as the saying goes, when you least expect it, expect it. Oh yes, and don't take it out. I'm having too much fun."

Alice smiled. She was having fun, too. But she also realized that a few more flips of that switch and she would come in front of all these people. And she didn't usually climax quietly. "Be nice baby, or I'll embarrass both of us," she said.

Mario looked down at the huge tent in the front of his slacks. "Me, too."

The next two hours were torture for Alice and Mario. Each knew what would happen after the party, but they couldn't leave until at least eleven. Twice, Mario caught his wife's eye and slipped his hand into his jacket pocket. A quick flip of the switch and he could watch Alice's body jump. He knew exactly how hot she was and he could almost see her erect nipples through her wool dress. He only left the machine on for a few seconds, but it was enough to keep both of them on edge.

"John," he said to his boss just after eleven o'clock, "Alice really isn't feeling well this evening. I'm going to take her home."

John Harper's gaze found Alice in animated conversation with his wife. "She looks fine to me."

Mario reached into his pocket. "It comes in waves." He flipped the switch and the two men watched his wife suddenly become distracted.

"Of course," John said. "You must take her home." As Mario moved across the room, Mr. Harper called after him, "And I hope she feels better."

Smiling, Mario got their coats and escorted Alice to their car. She laughed as he related the method he had used to convince his boss of Alice's supposed illness.

"You didn't," Alice said as Mario drove toward their house.

"I did indeed." He arrived at their house and pulled the car into the garage, then closed the mechanical door with the remote switch. "Now," he said as he grabbed his wife's seat belt and used it to hold her tightly in her seat, "let's stay here for a few minutes."

"But the house is empty. Why here?"

"Because I want to try an experiment. Don't move." He reached into his pocket and pulled out the remote control. "Is that thing still inside you?"

"Yes," Alice said, watching his hand.

"You tried to use it to drive me crazy, didn't you?"

"Yes."

"Well, two can play at that game." He held the switch in front of her face and, while she watched, flipped it again. "Let's see how long it takes. I want to watch you come."

Her eyes lit up. "Oh Mario, that's cruel." She felt the hum in her pussy.

"It certainly is, but that's the punishment you deserve, I think."

"If you twist the top there, it changes the speed of the vibrations." Alice was climbing and loving it.

"Really." Mario slowly twisted the top and Alice could feel the hum change in her pussy. "Maybe you should tell me which speed you like best."

Alice swallowed hard. She was going to come, but she wanted to put it off as long as possible.

"Trying to hold back?" Mario grinned at Alice's startled expression. "I know you very well, and you know I love to watch you get higher and higher. I can read your excitement in every line of your body." He twisted the control rhythmically back and forth. "You're really having a difficult time holding back, aren't you?" When Alice remained silent, Mario said again, "Aren't you?"

"Yes," Alice said through gritted teeth.

"Well, I want you to come now! Spread your legs."

Still restrained by her tight dress and her seat belt, Alice parted her knees as best she could. Mario reached between her thighs and tapped his wife lightly on her clit.

She came. She couldn't help it. Hard, hot waves of climax engulfed her body and she screamed, "Oh God." Her body writhed as she drew the sensations more deeply into her. Finally, she took the control and turned the vibrator off. "Upstairs. I want you to fuck me good."

"Oh darling," Mario said.

The two left a trail of discarded clothing through the house, and by the time they reached the bedroom, they were both naked, except for Alice, who still wore her panties to hold the vibrator inside. She dropped onto the bed on her back and Mario stretched out beside her. He reached between her spread legs and touched the flat end of the vibrator. "Would it feel good if I turned that on again, or would it be too much?"

"I'm not sure." She grinned. "Maybe you'd better try and see."

Mario played with the control until Alice's hips thrashed and her back arched. "My turn," he said, pulling her panties off and withdrawing the vibrator. His cock felt hard as steel as he drove it into his wife's drenched pussy.

"More," Alice yelled as she felt another orgasm building. "Fuck me harder."

Mario grabbed Alice's thighs and pushed them upward against her chest. Then, pinning her legs, he pressed against her and plunged his cock into her wide-open pussy. Mario could hold back no longer. "Now!" he yelled as he felt semen spurt deep into Alice's pussy.

"Yes, now!" she screamed, and they came together.

Later they lay together holding hands. "That doesn't often happen," Mario said, "us coming together, I mean."

"No, it doesn't." Alice pulled the edge of the quilt over them. "And it was amazing."

"I never thought I'd say this," Mario said, laughing, "but I can't wait until the Harpers' next party."

TRY SOMETHING NEW: ORDERING FROM CATALOGS

I've mentioned erotic toys previously, and in a few stories, couples have played with sexual props. Since money may be a bit easier now that the kids are gone, you may want to consider ordering from a sex catalog.

First, where can you find such catalogs? There are usually advertisements for the larger companies in the back of women's magazines. As I write this, I'm looking at the latest issue of *Cosmopolitan*, and there are ads for the Xandria Collection, Adam and Eve, and several smaller companies. In addition, there is a catalog of information included in my book *Come Play With Me*, and I have gathered a collection of "web pages for shoppers" on my web site, found at http://www.JoanELloyd.com.

Let's talk about those heavily advertised sexual aids and vitamins for a moment.

A warning: To the best of my knowledge, there are no over-the-counter aphrodisiacs that will make her "unable to resist you," and no pheromone products that will make you "irresistible to women." Read all the advertisements with skepticism.

Aphrodisiacs and other types of sex drugs have been the stuff of fantasies since the first cavewoman said, "Not tonight, Og, I have a headache." Throughout the ages and all over the world, everything from oysters and grapes to animal testicles and powdered rhinoceros horns have been sold and consumed to increase sexual prowess. More recently, fads that have swept the sexual world ranged from aspirins mixed in Coke to green M&M's. In most cases, if they worked at all, what worked was the power of the mind, not the power of the product.

Many people believe that so-called recreational drugs can increase orgasmic potential. With many drugs, just the opposite is the case. The opiates, opium derivatives like heroin, actually decrease sexual function and can inhibit erections. Some claim that cocaine enhances the sexual experience, but studies have found that this is not the case. A moderate amount of alcohol does induce relaxation, but that's the only way it affects sexual performance. Marijuana is also relaxing in very small quantities, but in large amounts, it dissociates mind and body and isn't conducive to good sex. Many say that after smoking grass, they become so laid-back that they can't be bothered with sex at all. Ed smoked a joint a few times years ago and remembers that he got interested in intercourse, got ready, then forgot why he had been interested in the first place.

Prescription drugs do exist that have positive effects on sexual performance, but none comes without side effects, and such drugs should not be used without the advice of your doctor. One such drug is yohimbine, which has been around for many years and goes in and out of favor with doctors. The most recent studies seem to show that it is effective in about one-third of men with long-term erectile problems, but it seems to have no aphrodisiac effect on men with normal sexual function. Again, talk to your doctor.

Gels and such that are "guaranteed" to prolong your erection do just that. They do it, however, by numbing your penis to dilute the otherwise-overwhelming sensations. If that seems a good idea to you, they appear to be harmless, so give them a try.

I will discuss sexual dysfunction and impotence in the chapter entitled "We're Not Kids Anymore," so if you have such a problem, refer to that chapter and then check with your doctor. There are new medical treatments, ones that work. The products available through ads in magazines, however, aren't worth your money.

But with all these problems in finding a true "sex drug," the power of the mind mustn't be overlooked. If you believe you're the sexiest thing to come over the hill since James Dean or Elizabeth Taylor, then you will be sexier. If you and/or your partner believe that you're a male or female superstud, you will be. And if you can get your partner to believe that you've just given him or her a powerful aphrodisiac that will make him or her incredibly turned on, then it will happen that way.

A suggestion: Give your partner a small glass of colored water or a candy pill and then tell him that he's just ingested something that will make him unable to resist your slightest sexual desire. If the two of you are into it, it's a terrific game.

In the back of my issue of *Cosmo,* there is also an ad for Intimate Treasures, a company that assembles small ads for catalogs and charges a nominal fee for forwarding your name to one or more of the companies listed in their ad. They have catalogs for everything from XXX-rated movies of every description to books and magazines, toys, and clothing—in other words, anything you and your partner might want to use to spice up your sex life. I've sent orders to them and, for the most part, received what I requested. They will send you a listing of their catalogs if you write to Intimate Treasures, PO Box 77902, San Francisco, CA 94107-0902. If you're a computer person, they also have a site on the World Wide Web, located at http://www.intimatetreasures.com. And yes, it all does come in a plain wrapper.

What can you order? Almost anything, from homemade amateur X-rated videos to lingerie, from extrahigh-heeled shoes to nurses uniforms, from leather restraints to strawberry condoms. The prices range from quite low to exorbitant. But worth it? That, of course, depends on your pocketbook and desires.

How does one order? In most cases, you can order any product by mail, by phone, or by fax. Some even have E-mail addresses for faster service.

Sometimes just looking through the catalog will get the juices flowing. At other times, you can discover new things that can heat up your bedroom. In Craig and Sue's story, Sue has a real problem with the way she looks, as do most of us as we age. I'll cover the problems with body image more in the next chapter. For now, we can sympathize with Sue, but we can also delight in how groundless her fears proved to be.

CRAIG AND SUE'S STORY

Craig and Sue had been married for thirty-two years and, after twenty-eight years of parenting, each of their three children was finally in his or her own apartment. Their sons were both gainfully employed. Their daughter, Nancy, was married and a stay-at-home mom with two small children. Craig and Sue finally had the house to themselves, but although they had both been creative in the bedroom earlier in their marriage, over the years they had settled into a comfortable routine of plain vanilla sex once a week or so.

One week, their daughter and son-in-law left their two preschool children with Sue and Craig while they went on a cruise. Upon their return, they stayed for a few days and the six of them had a wonderful time together. The afternoon they left, Sue and Craig stretched out in the living room.

"I'm exhausted," Sue said. "I love my grandchildren, but they are a handful."

"Someone at the office said that grandchildren are a joy twice, once when they arrive and once when they go home." Craig saw the magazine in Sue's hand. "What's that?"

"Oh, I found this in the bathroom as the kids were packing. When I gave it to Nancy, she told me to keep it. Actually, she winked and told me she had lots more like it."

"What is it?" Craig asked.

Sue put the catalog in Craig's lap. "Take a look."

Craig stared at the scantily dressed model on the cover. "Oh," he said, turning to the first page. The catalog was filled with models dressed in almost nothing. As he turned the pages, the outfits got more and more outrageous. "Would you wear things like these?" he asked.

"Don't be silly."

Craig pointed to one of the pictures, a nubile young woman in a lace teddy with no bra cups. Her oversized breasts filled the openings. "I'd love to see you in something like this."

"You're being crazy. I haven't looked like that woman in thirty years. No wait, I take that back. Even thirty years ago, I didn't look like that."

"Of course you wouldn't look like that. You'd look like you." Seeing Sue's face, Craig let the subject drop. Later that afternoon, they made love with more passion than they had in a long time.

Several weeks later, Sue and Craig spent the evening relaxing on their bed watching *Some Like It*

Hot on a movie channel. As the movie ended, Craig took the remote and turned off the TV. Without a word, he went to the closet and pulled out a brown paper–wrapped package. He dropped in on the bed beside his wife. "Open it. It's for you."

"How come?" Sue asked. "It's not my birthday or anything."

"I know. Can't a husband buy something for his wife every now and then?"

"You know what they say about gift horses," Sue said, ripping the paper off the moderate-sized package. When she had exposed the box inside, she pulled off the cover. Inside was a black lace one-piece stretchy leotard, obviously bought from the catalog her children had left. "Oh Craig." What could she say? Without realizing what she was doing, she glanced at her almost completely flat chest.

Craig walked around the bed and placed his fingers beneath Sue's chin, lifting her face to look at him. "Look, baby. I've had that in the closet for weeks, waiting for the right time to give it to you. I looked at Marilyn in that movie and I just wanted to see you in this."

"But I'm no Marilyn Monroe." Her sense of the ridiculous came to the fore. "I'm closer to the president, *James* Monroe."

Not allowing her to divert him, he continued, "I know how you feel about your body and you're wrong. That's all there is to it."

Craig watched his wife's muscles tighten. "Oh Craig," she said, tears welling in her eyes.

"Baby, believe me. You think you're old and skinny and flat-chested. But—"

Sue interrupted. "But I am. The only time I had any

tits at all was when I was pregnant. I'm fifty-three." She found herself getting angry. "I'm old, way beyond this stuff. Oh Craig, how could you humiliate me like this?" Tears ran down her cheeks.

"I would never do anything to upset you like this, darling. I just saw this in the book and I so much wanted to see you in it. I think you're hot and sexy, that's all." He held the cat suit up and looked at her through the lace. "And it makes me hot to think of you enticing me with this thing on."

Sue swiped away her tears and looked at her husband's face. He really meant what he had said, she realized. He really thought she would look sexy in this ridiculous outfit. "You're serious," she said.

"I am." He took her hand and guided it to the swelling in his pants. "It got deflated thinking that I hurt you, but it's here for you."

"Really?"

"Really. I like your tits. I love your body just the way it is, because it's *your* body." He paused, then said, "I want you to go into the bathroom and put this on. Please."

"But . . ."

"Baby, do it for me. Do it because I want to see you in that stretchy thing." When he saw her hesitate, he added again, "Please."

Reluctantly, Sue picked up the package and walked into the bathroom. How could he? she thought. Didn't he understand? She pulled off her jeans and shirt and stepped out of her underpants. "No bra," she muttered, looking at her almost nonexistent breasts, "because there are no tits." She looked at the rest of her body. Not an ounce of fat anywhere. I look like a prepubescent boy, she thought, with old flabby skin. That person who said that you could never be too thin must never have been skinny. She ran her palms over her ribs and angular pelvic bones. Then she slid her fingers through her salt-and-pepper pubic hair. "It was bad enough to go gray," she muttered, "but when my pubic hair went gray, that was the final insult."

"Honey," the gentle voice came through the bathroom door. "Please."

Sue closed her eyes and pulled the suit up her legs and over her hips. She gasped when she noticed that the crotch was split.

Wiggling into the rest of the suit, she said, "Did you look at the picture of this thing carefully?"

"Not really. Why?"

She pushed her arms into the long lacy sleeves and adjusted the low V neck. "Well, let's just say it's not subtle." The lacy weave had been arranged so that there was lace around her breasts, but her nipples were clearly exposed. In the same way, her pubic mound was easily visible.

"When do I get to see?" Craig asked through the door.

"You asked for it," Sue said, reaching for the doorknob. With shaking hands, she squared her shoulders, turned the knob, and opened the door.

"Holy shit," Craig said, his eyes widening. "You look sensational."

"I do not," Sue said, "but thanks for saying it."

"Hush," Craig said. "I don't care how you think you look. Get over here!"

Sue looked at her husband, openmouthed. He was looking at her like a piece of chocolate cake that he was about to devour. And he had never spoken to her that way before, either. Astonished, she found that she liked it. She thought about the way she must look in the suit, but the look on Craig's face banished all negative thoughts. "You want me, come and get me," she said, suddenly brave.

A grin slowly spread over Craig's face. He reached out and grabbed his wife's wrist. "God, you look sexy in that thing." He yanked and Sue tumbled onto the bed. Craig found her mouth with his and kissed her deeply. He couldn't keep his hands still, rubbing and stroking Sue's body through the lace of the suit. He pinched her nipples, then sucked on them through the almost nonexistent material.

While Sue watched, he stood up and pulled off his clothes. His cock was harder than she had seen it in a long time. He lay beside her, on his side, propped on his elbow. "You look good enough to eat," he said, nibbling on her neck, her lips, her ears, her breasts. He placed his hand flat on her stomach, then slowly slid it lower, insinuating one finger between her thighs. When he felt her wet, springy hair, he looked into her eyes. Surprised, he said, "Hey, this thing has no crotch."

"I noticed," Sue said, spreading her thighs.

"I did, too," he said, rolling on top of her. "I don't want to wait." He used his hand to rub her pussy, then guided his cock inside her waiting body.

"It feels funny to have you inside me while I still have clothes on."

Craig moved sinuously against the lace of the suit. "Feels kinky, but good." They stroked and caressed while both Sue and Craig got increasingly excited. Finally, with a few last thrusts, Craig came, then rubbed Sue's body the way he knew she liked until she, too, was satisfied.

"I love you in that suit," Craig said later.

"Me, too," she said. And she suddenly realized that she actually meant it.

My first erotic novel, *Black Satin,* came out in June of 1995. It is a story about two very high-class call girls who operate out of a brownstone in Manhattan. Several months after the book's publication, I got a wonderful letter from a man who had been introduced to the adventures of Carla and Ronnie in a most unusual way. A contractor, he had been summoned to the home of a couple who wanted a room constructed in their home that would provide the freedom to explore sexual adventures the way Carla and Ronnie did in their brownstone. His clients had given him a copy of the book to take home, and after reading it, he moved a few walls and created a secret room for the couple, complete with a hidden entrance.

Dean and Norma created a similar room and, with a now-empty nest, creative minds, and a bit of cash, lived their deepest desires. Notice that these toys came from the hardware store, not a catalog.

DEAN AND NORMA'S STORY

After the last of Dean and Norma's five children left home, the two lovers spent several months working on plans to rearrange the upstairs of their large house. They wanted a room for their unusual kind of fun and games, but one that no one would know about. With the help of an understanding contractor and some cleverly rearranged walls, they created a separate, windowless room with an entrance through the back of Dean's closet. Soundproofed, well lit, and with a separate heating system, the creatively decorated "playroom," as it became known, was finally completed one Friday in February. Although they had seen the room throughout its construction, Dean and Norma had denied themselves the pleasures of using it. Therefore, that weekend was to be their first time.

"I know what I want to do tonight," Dean said as they sipped an after-dinner drink. He gazed at the ceiling as Norma replied, "Anything you want, baby."

Norma enjoyed it when Dean occasionally took complete charge of their lovemaking. They didn't play games like that often, but tonight it seemed like the most exciting way to christen the new room.

"Anything?" Dean said.

"Absolutely anything. I am your servant for the evening." She bowed her head and assumed a subservient posture, a position that she knew would encourage her husband to allow his imagination to run wild. Through lowered lashes, she watched a grin spread across Dean's face.

"Wait here for ten minutes. Then dress in old clothes that you don't care about and I'll send for you."

For ten minutes, Norma sat in the living room, listening to her husband rattle around upstairs. It was strange to hear closet doors and dresser drawers opening and closing, furniture moving, then footsteps, then suddenly nothing as Dean entered the new soundproofed environment. As the hand on her watch crawled, Norma found herself getting very turned on. Although she had no clear idea of what Dean had in mind, she knew it would end with incredible sex.

At the end of the prescribed ten minutes, Norma climbed the stairs and changed her clothes. Following Dean's instructions, she dressed in a paint-splattered jogging suit, old underwear, and an old pair of socks and tennis shoes. Then she sat on the bed to wait for her husband's summons.

After five more minutes of tense waiting, she heard Dean's voice. "Come in here, Norma."

Norma opened Dean's closet door and saw that the door to the new room stood open. She entered and closed it behind her. The room was wonderful. Three walls were covered with a soft beige leather wall covering; the fourth was mirrored, concealing wide closet doors. The floor was thickly carpeted in deep green and the ceiling was covered in white tiles, with translucent panels for lights. There were also spotlights in several places.

"Take off your shoes and socks first," Dean said, a broad grin lighting up his face. "This carpet feels wonderful on bare feet."

While doing as he suggested, Norma looked at the full-length terry-cloth robe he wore. She wiggled her naked toes in the deep pile, then said, "You're right. This feels decadent."

"Now, come over here," Dean said, taking her hand. He led her to an upholstered bench he had placed in the center of the room. "I want to do something new in honor of this new room, but I want to know whether you trust me."

"Trust you? Of course."

"I will stop anything at any time if you don't want to play anymore. Clear?"

"Of course."

"And you'll tell me to stop if you want me to?"

Norma wondered at all this preparation, but she knew she did trust Dean implicitly, and she couldn't imagine anything he might do that she wouldn't like. However, she said, "I will tell you to stop if I don't like something."

"Promise?"

"Wow. With all this buildup, you've gotten me very curious."

"Promise."

"I promise. What are we going to do?"

"I want to tie you up."

Norma's knees shook. Dean had taken charge of their lovemaking several times and she had found herself incredibly aroused by being told what to do. Together, they had read stories about lovers tying each other up, but they had never tried it. She looked into Dean's eyes. "All right."

"I've always wanted to do this, and our playroom gives me the freedom to tell you. But I don't want you to do it just for me, but because you find the idea intriguing, too." Dean took Norma's hand. "Do you?"

Norma was trembling. She never believed her husband would try anything like this. She realized that her nipples were hard and her pussy was very wet. She lowered her eyes. "Yes," she whispered.

Dean crossed to one of the mirrored closets. He opened one of the doors and withdrew a small paper bag. "I got these several months ago. From the beginning of the design of this room, I had a picture of you in my mind, and, well . . . Hold out your arms."

As Norma extended her arms, Dean took two leather straps from the bag. "These are actually dog collars, but they will do just fine, I think." He fastened one collar around each of Norma's wrists. "Now for the legs." He pulled two more collars from the bag and fastened one around each of Norma's ankles.

"Now what?" Norma asked softly.

"Lie on the bench the long way, on your belly."

Norma did as she had been told and watched as Dean threaded a long rope through the rings on the collars, then tied her wrists and ankles to the legs of the bench. When he was done, she heard him sigh. "Oh baby," he said. "I pictured this so often."

"I'm sorry you waited so long."

"How does it feel to be tied down like that?"

"There was a moment when it felt scary," Norma admitted.

Dean immediately bent over and reached for the rope. "I'll untie you."

"Don't," Norma said. "I said it was momentary. When that passed, it felt thrilling."

"Can you get loose?"

"No."

"Try. I want to watch."

Norma wiggled. She could slide the ropes up and down the legs of the bench, but she couldn't get free.

"Good. I like to see you like that," Dean said, his breathing rapid. "Can I go further?"

"I agreed I would tell you to stop if I didn't like something."

"Are you sure?"

Norma relaxed her entire body, allowing her arms and legs to hang limply and her head to fall against the edge of the bench. "Yes," she purred.

She heard rustling sounds and watched as Dean undressed. She saw that he was naked beneath the robe, his erection ready for the games to come. Then she felt a cloth tied across her eyes. "I want you unable to see," she heard Dean say. "Just remember the sight of my naked body, and how hot I am for you. Does that feel sexy?"

Deprived of her sense of sight, Norma panicked. "No. Yes. I don't know." It was sexy, she realized. "Yes. It's sexy. Very sexy."

"Good."

Norma heard noises from behind her, then felt Dean's hands on one leg. "These clothes are in the way," he said. "I have big scissors here and I'm going to make you all naked."

Norma jumped as the cold steel of the blade of the scissors touched her calf. Slowly she heard and felt the legs of her jogging pants being cut up the back to the waist.

"Now these," Dean said as he cut her panties. Then slowly, he rubbed the cold handles of the scissors over Norma's buttocks. "Feel the cold?"

Norma shivered. "Yes. I feel it." She felt the cold, smooth handles being rubbed over her inner thighs and then caressing her overheated pussy. "So cold."

"Let's warm things up a bit." He left her momentarily; then Norma felt heat on her ass. "I turned on a spotlight so it shines on your beautiful buns. Can you feel the warmth?"

"Oh yes."

"How does it feel on your pussy?"

Norma spread her knees slightly so the heat flowed to her crotch. "It's erotic feeling heat like that."

"Umm, good." Then she felt Dean's hands knead her buttocks and then he kissed and licked the smooth skin there. "You have such a beautiful ass," he purred. The shears snipped up the center of the back of the jogging top, then down each arm. He cut the back and straps of her bra with loud snaps of the scissors.

Now she lay on the remnants of her clothes, but her back was completely naked. She moaned from the excitement. She spread her knees as best she could to open her pussy to the heat and for her husband. "Not so fast," Dean said. "I know your pussy must be so hot and needy, but I'm not ready yet."

Norma heard some unidentifiable sounds, then felt something icy cold on her back. "When I bought the collars, I bought some chains, too—heavy, cold metal chains. He lifted her chest and placed a piece of the chain under her, against her heated breasts. "Just feel that." Then he wound the chain around her waist, under the bench, and fastened it somehow.

Norma couldn't hold her hips still. She was tied, blindfolded, now chained, and she was as hot as she had ever remembered. She wanted Dean's big cock filling her pussy. "Please," she moaned. "Please."

"No. Not yet. Although it's killing me not to fuck you right now, I want to go further. I want to make this into the picture I've had in my head since we began planning this room." He put a large bell in her hand. "Drop this or ring it if you want me to stop anything. I want to gag you so I can hear you moan but not speak. May I?"

Gag me? Could she? She wanted what Dean wanted, of course, but she knew that this had to be a mutual decision. She shook the bell in her hand.

"I'll stop now," Dean said, "and untie you. Is that what you want?"

She held the bell still. "No," she whispered.

"Are you as hot as I am?" Dean rubbed one finger up the inside of her thigh, to her steamy pussy.

"Yes," she said, trembling, "I am."

"May I go further?"

"Yes," she said.

She felt a piece of cloth being stretched across her mouth, then tied behind her head. She groaned at the helpless yet terribly exciting feeling. She could not see, could not speak.

"Ring the bell, so I know you can," Dean said, and she did. "Good." He moved her body slightly and stuffed a pillow beneath her lower belly. "I want to build a table that's like this, only higher, with rings, so I can tie you in different positions. God, you're so beautiful this way." Slowly, he inserted one finger into his wife's sopping cunt and felt her hips reach for him. As she wiggled, he slapped her hard across the rump.

"Ring the bell if you want me to stop."

Norma did want him to stop. He had slapped her in the heat of passion occasionally before, but this time he had hurt her. As she shifted her hand to ring the bell, the sting joined the spotlight's deep warmth and spread through her loins. She moaned through the cloth in her mouth. When he slapped her again, she rang the bell.

"Okay," he said, "no more. Shall I untie you? Ring the bell if you want me to stop everything." She did not.

"Your cheek is so red from my hand." He caressed the reddened area softly; then Norma felt one hand on each cheek, caressing and massaging, his thumbs coming close to her swollen lips but not touching her. Norma moved her hips, reaching for his fingers. She had to have something fill her pussy.

"Please," she said, her words muffled by the gag in her mouth.

"Oh yes," Dean said. "I think it's time."

There were some sounds; then Norma felt the tip of Dean's cock rub against her clit. Over and over he rubbed, until she thought she would climax from that sensation alone. Then he moved, entering her hungry pussy from behind, using his thumbs to stroke her clit. She wanted to reach down and rub her body to push her over the edge, but she was too well tied. She tamped down her impatience and savored the waiting, combining the sensations of blindness and powerlessness. I can't move, she told herself. I can't stop him from doing whatever he likes. She was in heaven.

As Dean's cock slowly alternately entered and withdrew, and as his fingers rubbed her, Norma knew she couldn't wait any longer. The climax overtook her, bursting behind her blindfolded eyes like all the colors of the rainbow. She screamed as Dean growled his own release. He collapsed on her naked back on top of the chains and lay there for a long time. Then he untied all the fastening and the two lay side by side on the carpet.

"Oh sweet," Dean said. "That was so much better than any fantasy."

Norma curled against Dean's side, her head on his shoulder. "It's never been any better for me, either."

"This room brings out the beast in me," he said, a note of timidity in his voice.

"I love that in a man," Norma said. "It was terrific."

"Was it really terrific for you?"

Norma playfully smacked Dean's shoulder. "It was fantastic. Except for that last slap."

"I'm so sorry about that," Dean said.

"Don't be. The first one surprised me, and that was erotic."

"It was?"

Norma understood her husband's need for reassurance. "It was. And I'd like you to try something like that again. Just not so hard."

Dean looked into his wife's eyes. "You don't really mean that, do you?"

"I made you a promise that I wouldn't ever do anything 'just for you,' and I won't."

"I love you," Dean said.

"I love you, too. And," she said, pausing, "I love this room."

As I think you now understand, an empty nest is what you make it. If you like, you can create a playful atmosphere where anything is possible, where long-secret dreams can come true.

AGELESS FANTASIES

The first of the fantasies in this section involves a husband who fantasizes about making love with his wife and her best friend. There are two issues that should be discussed here: fantasizing about someone other than your spouse and threesomes.

Most of us have had images of making love with someone other than our mate at one time or another. It may be your next-door neighbor, the new typist on the fifth floor, Sharon Stone, or Sean Connery. There's nothing wrong with these dreams, and frequently they can get your juices started during an evening with your partner. And often your dream partner changes identity, depending on what movie you've seen most recently. In the *Bonanza* days, my fantasy partner used to change from Michael Landon to Pernell Roberts to Lorne Greene to Dan Blocker and back again, depending on the nature of that week's episode.

Is this type of fantasy bad? Jimmy Carter said that he had "sinned in his mind" from time to time. I don't think we can sin in our thoughts, only in our actions. I never had any intention of making love to anyone other than my husband, but the fantasies were exciting nonetheless.

Threesomes and moresomes are the basis of many fantasies. I've received several letters from women who are dismayed at their husband's suggestion that they act out a threesome. I respond to all these letters with the same warning: Don't. Bringing a third person into a relationship is extremely risky. There are always jealousies, comparisons, and bruised egos, no matter how careful and caring the three people are. In my opinion, this is a fantasy to tell midnight stories about but not to act upon.

With that in mind, here are two more ageless fantasies.

RICK'S FANTASY

Rick and Cathy had been married for almost ten years and their sex life was creative and satisfying. However, like most lovers, Rick had a very private sexual fantasy, one that involved Lynn, Cathy's best friend. Sometimes, in the middle of the night, he would awaken hard and hurting, the image of Lynn in his mind. Sometimes he would fall back to sleep, and sometimes he would gently awaken Cathy and make wonderful love to her. Occasionally, he would go into the bathroom and masturbate, the picture of Lynn's body in his mind. He would never dream of acting out his fantasy, and he didn't even like Lynn particularly, but it was her body that was the stuff his dreams were made of.

Cathy had short curly brown hair, large brown eyes, and a voluptuous body, with large, soft breasts and a lush figure that Rick loved to caress, kiss, and lick. Lynn was a redhead, tiny and almost painfully thin, with a chest that was almost flat and boyish contours that Rick dreamed about. His dreams were usually the same.

"Honey," Rick said as he closed the front door behind him, "I'm home."

"We're in the kitchen," Cathy called.

We? Rick put his briefcase in the den with his jacket and tie, then wandered into the kitchen. The sweet smell of cooking strawberries assaulted him. Cathy and Lynn were just cleaning up, now surrounded by dozens of jars of freshly made ruby red jam. The two women were filling the sink with sticky-looking bowls, pots, and spoons. Empty farm-stand containers littered the counters.

"Hi, Rick," Lynn said. "We really did a number on the kitchen, but we couldn't resist these berries." She looked around the kitchen as Cathy began to fill the sink with soapy water. "Ah. Here they are," she said, finding a few leftover berries in one container. "Taste."

Lynn held one large, luscious berry by the husk and extended it toward Rick's mouth. He parted his lips and, with Lynn's fingers just brushing his mouth, took a large, juicy bite. As he bit, his lips brushed her fingertips. He gazed deeply into her eyes. "Wonderful," he whispered.

Lynn walked toward the refrigerator. "Strawberries go so well with champagne," she said, opening the door, "that we couldn't resist." She pulled a bottle of champagne from the refrigerator and refilled the two glasses that sat on the counter. "Want some?"

Cathy, who had been silent since Rick's arrival home, giggled.

"Sure." Rick got a flute from the cabinet and Lynn filled it with bubbling golden liquid. "That bottle's still almost full," he said. "You haven't had much yourselves." He walked over and kissed his wife on the back of her neck.

"Actually," Cathy said, turning so her lips were close to Rick's, "that's our second bottle. We're pretty pickled."

Rick couldn't resist licking a sticky drop of jam from the corner of Cathy's mouth.

"And horny, too," Cathy added.

"Okay," Lynn said. "This is my cue to go home to my empty house." Outspoken and a free spirit, Lynn had been divorced for several years, and although she dated frequently, she still enjoyed being single.

"Actually," Cathy said, "I think Rick would love it if you stayed." She kissed his surprised mouth. "Wouldn't you like that?"

Rick could only stare.

"Now don't tell me you don't fantasize about Lynn," Cathy said. "I don't mind. Really."

"I don't take advantage of drunken ladies," Rick said, sad that his honor wouldn't let him take advantage of the situation.

Lynn took the half-eaten strawberry and dipped it

into her glass. "We've been talking a lot about you recently, and not just when we're a bit inebriated. Cathy says that you've got the hots for me." She held the dripping strawberry toward Rick. "Want another nibble?"

Rick allowed Lynn to fill his mouth with the champagne-soaked berry.

"Do you really think about me?" she continued.

Rick couldn't deny the obvious. "Yes," he said simply.

Quickly, Lynn pulled her T-shirt off over her head. Needing no bra, she was gloriously naked beneath. "I can't imagine anyone wanting these flat little titties," she said, cupping her tiny breasts. "Men always want handfuls." She walked over and pulled Cathy's shirt off. Cathy's large breasts filled the cups of her bra and bulged over the tops. "Like these."

She unhooked Cathy's bra and pulled it off, allowing her large breasts their freedom.

Rick's mind was boggled. Lynn had turned so the two women were standing facing him, side by side. Here were two wonderfully desirable women, naked to the waist, standing in his kitchen, looking at him hungrily.

"Now be serious," Lynn said over Cathy's giggles. "Wouldn't you much rather have Cathy's tits in your mouth than mine?" When Rick didn't move, Lynn continued: "We've been wondering which tits you'd prefer to suck, haven't we?" Cathy nodded silently. "So come here and do a taste test."

Rick looked at the breasts, one set large, soft, and familiar, the other small, tight, and excitingly strange, with large, pointed, completely erect nipples. Almost numb, Rick crossed the kitchen. "Don't be shy," Lynn goaded.

Rick bent over and took his wife's breast in his mouth. He felt the nipple harden as he licked and suckled. He moved to Lynn's and reveled in the unusual feel of flat, tight flesh and her unusually large nipple. "That's it, baby," Lynn said. "Have a good taste."

"Mine are better," Cathy said through her laughter, dipping her finger in some leftover jam and spreading it on her nipple. "Try this." She guided Rick's mouth to her sticky globe.

Rick tasted his wife's skin through the red goo, aware that Lynn was picking up a finger full of jam and covering her breast with it.

Soon Cathy and Lynn's chests were sticky and well sucked. "You both taste delicious," Rick pronounced. He soaked a dish towel in warm water and slowly washed both women, sad that this erotic interlude was over.

"I wonder about pussies," Cathy said. "Would we taste different there?" In a flash, she had stripped off her shoes, socks, jeans, and panties. She sat on the counter and spread her knees. "Taste me."

So hungry that he was nearly senseless, Rick buried his face in his wife's pussy, licking her familiar juices. He lapped at her wetness, sampling the delights he always found there—her swollen outer and inner lips, her hard clit, her wide-open slit. "Oh yes," he heard Cathy moan. "Taste me good."

After a few minutes of enjoyment, Cathy pushed Rick's head away. "Now taste Lynn."

Rick looked deeply into his wife's eyes. "You know where this is heading, don't you? Are you sure?"

Cathy kissed him deeply. "You taste of me," she said, smiling. "And yes, I'm completely sure. This is something for you, and for me, too."

"We've talked a lot about you, Rick, and this," Lynn

said, "and we decided to take advantage of an opportunity for both of us to love you together, if the situation presented itself. But we also agreed that anyone can say no at any time."

Cathy looked seriously into Rick's eyes. "I'm not too smashed to know that this is something I want to share with you and Lynn. I say yes."

Lynn pulled off the remainder of her clothes and hiked herself onto the counter. She moved thigh-to-thigh with Cathy and spread her legs. "Ever taste a red-head?"

Rick was beyond coherent thought. He placed his hands on Lynn's tight, muscular thighs and slid his thumbs toward her flame-colored pussy hair. He looked into her eyes and relished her heavy-lidded expression. His thumbs reached their destination: Lynn's soaked pussy. As he parted her lips, he noticed that Lynn trimmed her pubic hair so the outer strands were long but the ones against her inner lips were very short. "Yes, Rick," she purred. "Do it. Taste me."

Rick buried his face in her bush, inhaling her musky fragrance, so different from his wife's. He flicked her clit with the tip of his tongue, then lapped the length of her slit.

He felt Cathy take his right hand and place it in her crotch, using his index finger to rub her erect nub. He used his left hand to rub Lynn the same way. Each woman allowed her head to fall back and her eyes to close, totally involved in the sucking and rubbing. Rick moved back and forth between the women, lapping, rubbing, sucking. Then he moved one finger toward the opening of each slit, simultaneously entering each woman with one finger.

It became a game. Could he bring each woman to

orgasm at the same moment? He fingered the two different pussies, gauging the height of arousal of each woman. He slowed, then speeded up. With one, he pulled his hand back while he entered the other with two, then three fingers. He watched them, seated on the kitchen counter, eyes closed, mouths open, climbing higher and higher.

He knew when his wife was close, and he hoped that Lynn was nearing climax also. While he fucked Cathy's cunt with three fingers, he drew Lynn's clit into his mouth, sucking rhythmically, pulling both women toward orgasm. "Yes, baby," Cathy moaned. "Like that."

"Oh Rick," Lynn whispered. "So good."

"Now," Cathy screamed, and he felt her muscles contract on his hand.

"Right now," Lynn yelled, pussy juice flowing into his mouth.

He could feel both women come, and, still lapping and finger-fucking, he grinned.

While the two women recovered, Rick removed all his clothing. He stood in the middle of the kitchen, his fully erect naked cock extending from his groin, and looked at his wife and her friend as they eyed him hungrily. "Let's do our own taste test," Lynn said, dropping from the counter to the floor. She scooped up a palmful of jam and rubbed it on Rick's cock.

As Cathy's bare feet touched the floor, she suggested, "You lick that side and I'll lick this one. Then we can change sides and see whether there's any difference."

The women motioned Rick toward the counter and he sat on the cool Formica. His overheated balls were against the cold surface and his cock stood straight up from his pubic hair. Cathy bent over and licked the length of his shaft on one side, and Lynn did the same on the other.

Rick was beyond control. Two hot mouths lapped at his cock; two tongues licked the length of him. One hot hand slid between his thighs and cupped his balls, and from his angle, he couldn't tell whose it was. He looked down at two heads, one brown, one red, bobbing over his cock. He closed his eyes as one mouth surrounded him, taking him deep inside its wet cavern. A tongue licked one flat male nipple. A finger rubbed the sensitive area at the base of his balls.

He moaned when he could take no more; then semen erupted and filled the mouth on his prick. Lynn's? Cathy's? He neither knew nor cared. He just kept spewing come.

When he finally opened his eyes, both women were getting dressed. "An interesting exercise," Lynn said.

Cathy giggled. "And so educational."

Slowly, Rick got down from the counter and stepped into his slacks, shaking his head. "I don't believe what just happened," he said.

"You know," Lynn said, "you're just as talented as Cathy said you were. And she really can brag." She grabbed her pocketbook from a chair and walked toward the front door. "You really are terrific, Rick. Let's do this again soon."

Rick looked at his wife questioningly. She smiled back at him. "Oh yes," she said loudly. "We will."

As Rick lay in bed, he felt Cathy turn over and cuddle against him. He knew he would never really make love with Lynn, but it was a delightful fantasy. Suddenly, he felt a hand on his erect cock. "Dreaming about me again?" Cathy said, sliding down to take him in her mouth.

As his cock slid deeper into Cathy's throat, Rick no longer cared whom he had been dreaming about or why. He just enjoyed.

CLAIRE'S FANTASY

It was a hot, humid night and Claire needed a breath of air. The central air conditioning in the split-level house she and her husband, Glen, had rented for the summer had gone on the fritz, just at the beginning of a series of steamy July days. They had been sleeping in the family room, the coolest spot in the house, but tonight, rest had become impossible for her.

"The repairman will be there on Monday," the landlord had promised, but now it was Thursday night and the air conditioner was still dead.

Claire slipped a light cotton cover-up over her damp skin and opened the back door, leaving her husband asleep. She glanced back and watched the even rise and fall of his chest, his body illuminated by a shaft of moonlight through the open door. She smiled at the corner of a sheet he had pulled across his groin, conservative even in his sleep.

Sighing, Claire slipped out the door and walked through the backyard, wiggling her toes in the cool grass. She slid her hand under her long hair and lifted it from her overheated neck. Nothing seemed to cool her off. She approached the swing set that the landlord had installed for the previous tenant, lifted her dress to her waist, and sat down on the plastic swing strap. She took little backward steps until the swing was as far back as she could get it, then lifted her feet and spread her legs.

The feeling of the warm air rushing across her hot, wet skin as the swing swept forward was exhilarating. Back the swing flew, then rushed forward again, the wind between her spread legs incredibly erotic. She pumped her legs like she had as a child, but the feel of the plastic on her naked buttocks and the air on her skin was most assuredly a grown-up feeling. She let her head fall backward and closed her eyes.

She swung for several minutes, her eyes still closed, savoring her feelings. Suddenly, she felt the swing stop, held a few feet forward. Her eyes flew open and she looked into her husband's face.

"What a sight you make," he said, his voice hoarse.

A bit unsettled, she said, "It just felt so good."

"I could tell." He stood there holding the swing partway forward in its arc. "You look good enough to eat."

Claire wasn't sure she was hearing correctly. Did he mean that double entendre? He was usually so serious about lovemaking, preferring it in the bedroom, at night, in the traditional missionary position. She had wanted him to loosen up for a long time, so now she said, "So? What are you going to do about it?"

His hands on the plastic chains, Glen pulled the swing closer and pressed his open mouth against his wife's. Unable to hold her against him with his hands, he used the force of his kiss to pull her to him. Long moments passed, their mouths fused together under the moon-bright sky.

Claire wrapped her legs around Glen's waist and pressed her wet cunt against his bare belly, just above the jeans he had thrown on over his naked body.

"God, baby," he growled. "You will get yourself into a lot of trouble if you do that."

Claire was delighted at the way Glen was loosening up. How far could she push him? "What kind of trouble?" she teased.

"This kind," he snapped, letting the swing down into its resting position. He sat on the ground beneath the swing, his mouth at exactly the height of her pussy. He pressed his hands against her buttocks and held her body against his mouth. Like a man starving, he lapped at her wet flesh, stroking the length of her slit with the flat of his tongue. "Oh God," she moaned. "Oh God."

He licked, then sucked her engorged clit into his mouth and massaged the tip with his tongue. Rhythmically, he sucked, flicked, then released, until Claire felt her orgasm boil from low in her belly. "Don't stop," she yelled. "Oh God, don't stop." Over and over, he licked until, with her thighs tight against his head, he felt her climax.

While she was still coming, he quickly stood up and pulled down his jeans. He lifted her from the swing and set her on her feet on the grass. Almost unable to stand, Claire watched him sit on the swing, then motion to her to sit on his lap, facing him, her legs over his thighs. A bit awkwardly, she climbed over him and felt his cock against the entrance to her passage. "Do it," he groaned, and she lowered herself onto his shaft, burying it to his balls.

He moved his feet backward, lifting the swing, then let his feet go. The swing dropped, then rose like a pendulum. Back and forth they swung, Glen's cock buried in Claire's pussy. Screaming, Claire's orgasm began to peak again, continuing as Glen pulled the front of her sundress down and took a hard nipple in his mouth. Holding the plastic chains, sucking and swinging, he arched his back and erupted deep inside his wife's body. With a loud scream, Claire came again, as well.

Too exhausted to do anything but hold on and let the swing come to a stop, the two rested for long minutes. "Oh my God," Claire said finally. "That was amazing."

Eyes downward, Glen said, "I don't know what came over me."

Claire squeezed her vaginal muscles and giggled. "I know what came, all right."

"But I'm not like this," he said, his speech hesitant.

"You aren't usually," Claire said, sensing her husband's discomfort. "But this was sensational and I loved it."

"Really?" Glen said softly.

"Really. I have always wanted our lovemaking to be fun, spontaneous, and creative like this."

Glen looked at his wife, her body drenched with sweat, gleaming in the moonlight. "This certainly is creative. I was so hot, and I saw the door open, so I stepped outside for some air. When I saw you swinging, your body so beautiful in the moonlight, I just needed you like this."

Glen's voice suddenly interrupted her reveries. "Honey, are you out there?"

Claire opened her eyes and saw her husband wander out the back door. "I'm here."

"I am so hot," Glen said.

Claire smiled. "So am I. Come join me."

5 ❥
We're Not Kids Anymore

A seventy-three-year-old man is seated in his doctor's office after his semiannual physical. "You're in great shape," the doctor says. "Healthy and fit, for a man your age."

"That's wonderful, Doctor," the man answers. "And that's very good news, since I'm getting married next week."

The doctor leans across the desk and shakes the man's hand. "I'm so happy for you both," he says. "Tell me about her."

"Well," the man says, hesitating, "she's gorgeous and sexy, and she's twenty-seven."

The doctor clears his throat. "Well," he says. "You know you're no spring chicken. Sex . . . Well, you understand. . . . You might consider—to keep everyone happy, you know, sexually—you might take in a boarder."

The man thinks a moment, then says, "That might not be a bad idea."

Six months later, the two are again seated in

the doctor's office. "Marriage seems to agree with you," the doctor says. "I've never seen you healthier."

"Thanks," the man says. "And by the way, my wife's pregnant."

"Congratulations. I guess you followed my advice and took in a boarder."

"I did," the man says. "She's pregnant, too."

*M*any people, like the doctor in the story, have written sex off among older people. "Make the best of it," they say, "because the best of sex is behind you."

While I was listening to the Frank Sinatra song "It Was a Very Good Year" recently, I realized how pervasive that idea is. The song tells about the women with whom Frank had relationships at seventeen, twenty-one, and thirty-five. Now, he sings, in the autumn of my life, I look back and think about how good my life was. That's all well and good, but Frank, of all people, should know that it's not all over just because you're past sixty, or seventy, or eighty. As the old line says, "Just because there's snow on the roof doesn't mean the fire's out in the furnace." I can testify that my furnace—and Ed's, too—is still functioning perfectly, and I intend to keep it that way for a very long time. Maybe our days of hanging from the chandelier are over, but the days of good sex can continue as long as we want them to.

Allow me to introduce you to the role model for good sex in later years.

As an avocation, I am an emergency medical technician and I take ambulance calls with two local volunteer organizations. In my town, there are several residences for seniors, and, as you can well imagine, we get called there frequently. Recently, we got a call to respond to one of the residences to aid a man with a hip injury. I've changed the names to protect the delightfully guilty.

We arrived and were met at the door by one of the residence's senior administrators. "You'll find Mr. Smith in room one fourteen," he told us. "But please, be discreet."

"Is there a problem?" I said, wheeling the stretcher down the long hallway.

"Well, one fourteen isn't exactly his room."

Still puzzled, I looked at him while one of my partners began to snicker. "Oh," I said, comprehension dawning. "Is there a need for secrecy?"

"Well, no, not really. He and Ms. Jones are certainly consenting adults, since she's eighty-one and he's eighty-three. But I don't want it to set a bad example."

Bad example, I thought. It's a great example. However, I decided to tread gently. We arrived in the room and found Mr. Smith on the bed. "It doesn't hurt too much," he said, "but I can't seem to move."

Ms. Jones was seated in a chair, dressed in a chintz robe, looking very distraught. "I'm Barbara Jones, his er . . . friend. We were just, well, we were . . ."

"Don't worry, Ms. Jones," I said, "we'll take good care of him."

"Hey, Barbara," Mr. Smith said to Ms. Jones, "go ahead and tell 'em what we were doing. I'm damn proud of it. I gave it to you good, didn't I?"

Ms. Jones merely blushed and hugged her robe more tightly around her.

"Well, lady," he said to me, "I give as good as I get,

maybe better." He winked, then added, "What are you doing later?"

"My name's Joan," I told him with a grin, "and let's not worry about later right now."

Preserving what modesty we could, we examined Mr. Smith's naked body and concluded that he probably had indeed broken his hip. We carefully transferred him to our stretcher and covered him with a sheet and a light blanket. Then we wheeled him back down the hallway toward the main front room, through which we had to go to get to the front door and out to the waiting ambulance.

When we arrived in the main sitting room, several older women were waiting to wish Mr. Smith a speedy recovery. Suddenly, Mr. Smith whipped off the blanket and yelled, "Hey, ladies, who wants to see my injury?"

There were titters, giggles, and, from myself and my crew, hearty laughter.

Thank heavens this case isn't unusual. There was an article in the *New York Times* recently about a very prestigious senior residence facility in New York City that had issued a residents' bill of sexual rights. The men and women had the right to explicit material—books, movies, and the like—and they had the right to date, carry on, and such, as long as they did so without upsetting others.

It isn't that this hadn't been true in the past, but the facility was now openly admitting that their residents were, and had every right to be, sexual beings. How wonderful. And this is happening more and more as the population ages.

Sexual age discrimination occurs all over. Dozens of times a day, we are bombarded with this message: I'm still young and useful and sexual, but if I don't do what the commercial demands, I'll be old, dried-up, and useless.

"I'm over forty and I still look wonderful." First we are led to believe that the fact that she is over forty and hasn't fallen apart yet is simply due to the power of the advertiser's product. And, more important and more insidious, we are being told that if you don't look good, you're finished; your life is over.

If one more nubile twenty-five-year-old says, "I'm not going to age gracefully; I'm going to fight it all the way," I think I'll scream.

"For the young and the young at heart." I particularly hate that phrase; it's as though *old* is a dirty word.

Okay, let's get realistic. Aging does bring about many changes in our bodies. After menopause, a woman can have difficulty lubricating properly. Men can have problems with getting and maintaining an erection, and that erection may not be as hard as it once was. So what? We will get to specific problems and solutions later in this chapter, but it's that awful mental image of used-up, nonsexual people that I'm fighting first. You're older, not dead yet. Let's get together and stamp out pejorative phrases like "dried-up," referring in part to a lack of lubrication; "sexy senior," as if that's an oxymoron; and "dirty old man," as if it's worse to have sexy thoughts when you're older and supposed to be beyond that. Okay, I'll get down off my soapbox now.

Let's begin with one of the most basic problems that comes with aging: our body image. Although I'm discussing it here, body image can be a problem at any age, and I'm living proof.

As a young person, I had a Nose. Not a nose with a small *n* but a Nose with a capital letter. Actually, the rest of my face wasn't half-bad, but, as I saw it, who could ever know? My large nose overshadowed the rest of me. When I was beginning to think about boys, at about thirteen, I asked my mother if she thought I was pretty. She answered, "You're good-looking, Joan, and an attractive person. And you may not have as many first dates as some of your friends, but you'll have lots more second dates." That was nice, but not what a budding teenager wanted to hear.

Over the next year, I watched my pretty friends start to date. Me? Nothing. So my mother and I seriously considered plastic surgery. We talked about it and then finally visited a doctor and had an evaluation. I decided to have the surgery, and my mother backed me up. So, at fifteen, on the day after my graduation from high school, I had my Nose done.

It was a relatively simple procedure, and when I was wheeled down from the operating room, I was groggy but conscious. "I'm gorgeous," I said from below two black eyes and a swollen forehead. And I believed it. My whole personality had changed. I went from feeling like an insecure teenager to a self-proclaimed dazzler of members of the opposite sex. And it was a self-fulfilling prophesy. I began to date and I had an active social life throughout college, meeting, dating, and, I suppose, dazzling my future husband in the process.

Had I changed that much? No. Everyone said that after all the healing was complete, I looked like a well-retouched photograph of myself. But my feelings about myself had changed dramatically, and that was all that mattered. That was my first taste of the power that body image has on us—that time, for the better.

It wasn't all smooth sailing, however. My problems with body image surfaced again soon after the birth of my first daughter. When I got pregnant, I weighed only about 115, and at five seven, that wasn't really quite fleshy enough for my husband. "Maybe after you have the baby," he said at one point, "you could weigh a little more. I'd like a bit more meat on your bones." What could be better for a pregnant lady? French fries, hot fudge sundaes, and Milky Ways. Life was good.

My body changed dramatically almost immediately. In my first month of pregnancy, my bra size went from a 34B to a 36E. My husband was delighted, but I was less than thrilled. Not only did my clothes not fit properly but also I was extremely sore and uncomfortable. Despite my eating habits, however, I didn't gain scads of weight during my pregnancy—about twenty pounds, as I recall, six pounds twelve ounces of which I lost during childbirth. By the time of my visit to my obstetrician for my six-week checkup, I had lost most of the weight I had gained and was doing what I could to flatten my stomach. And, to my husband's disappointment and my very mixed feelings, I was back to my 34B bras.

My obstetrician gave me a thorough going-over and pronounced me healthy and ready for the first comfortable sex in fourth months and the first sex of any kind in eight weeks. "Okay," he muttered, "let me just make a few notes here." He mumbled as he scribbled on my chart. As I dressed, one muttered phrase leapt at me through the curtain: "Breasts, pendulous."

I looked down and saw that there was lots more skin than there was stuff to fill it up. Breasts, pendu-

lous. I looked in the mirror that covered one wall of
the dressing area and had to admit that he was right. I
drooped. I had a few stretch marks, an old but quite
large appendectomy scar, and pendulous breasts. I
was devastated.

I can't say it ruined my life. I returned to my ade-
quate, if uncreative, sex life without too much change
in my attitude. But many times as I dried after my
shower, I glanced in the bathroom mirror. Breasts,
pendulous. And I've been self-conscious ever since.

Let's talk about body image. Answer these four
questions for me—quickly and without censorship.

1. Thinking of yourself above the neck, what's your
   worst feature?
2. Thinking of yourself above the neck, what's your
   best feature?
3. Thinking of yourself below the neck, what's your
   worst feature?
4. Thinking of yourself below the neck, what's your
   best feature?

Don't read on until you've answered all four questions as honestly as you can.

Okay, now that you've got your answers firmly in
your mind, you can forget them. I don't care what your
responses were. What I'm more interested in is the
length of time it took for you to answer. I'll bet that if
you're honest with yourself, it was a lot easier and
faster to think of your worst features than your best.
We're conditioned that way. Find your imperfections
and work on them, we're told. Fix them. Diet, work
out, get plastic surgery, have liposuction. Use face
cream, eye cream, neck cream, hand cream, thigh

cream. Be beautiful and be happy. Be imperfect and be miserable. Well, if you weren't miserable before the commercials, you are now.

The kind of perfection the commercials and all the other subliminal gimmicks insist on is unattainable. There's always a bulge here, a hollow there, a wrinkle here, a pimple there. We can't win. Even those pictures on the front cover of *Cosmo* are carefully retouched.

I remember the heyday of *Charlie's Angels,* now newly popular in rerun. God, those women were fantastic. Gorgeous, smart, and good shots, too. I remember the incredible popularity of Jaclyn Smith, Kate Jackson, and Farrah Fawcett.

Then I read an interview with Farrah Fawcett, sex goddess for an entire generation of men, sex idol for a generation of women. In the article, she said she thought she had fat thighs. Fat thighs! I think that was the moment when I decided to try my best to resist the lure of physical perfection. It's not easy to weather the onslaught of the constant messages, and I admit that I still use face cream and hand cream, but the panic is muffled. I am what I am and I try to be happy with that. And, after all, my good skin, gray hair, and pendulous breasts are all a result of genes and nature and nothing more.

Here's something I want you to do. Take awhile and think of that part that you decided you're particularly happy with—the one above the neck and the one below—or select one now if you copped out on my little quiz. Go into the bathroom and look at yourself in the mirror if you need to. You may have to think for a while because you're not used to concentrating on your good parts. Your toes? Your fingernails? Your shoulders? Maybe it's your earlobes, or your hairline, or even your eyebrows. Pick one thing above the neck and one below it. Do it.

If you're like most of the rest of us, the last thing you look at when you leave a mirror is the one part of your body you're most unhappy with. You check the full-length mirror on the back of the bathroom door to assure yourself that your hips haven't expanded in the past fifteen minutes. You take one last look at your prominent chin or large ears when you finish shaving or complete your makeup.

Okay. Now, every time you leave a mirrored area, I want the last thing you look at to be that "best thing" of yours. Let your eyes linger just a split second on that one part of you that you're most happy with. Nice calves! Nice eyes! It won't create miracles, but it will change your perception just a bit.

I can give you women one suggestion about the way you look. Nothing makes a woman look more dated or more out of touch than her makeup. If you're still using heavy dark eyeliner the way you did twenty years ago, or still brushing on the light blue eye shadow, get one of the fashion-oriented magazines and look at the makeup ads carefully. Compare the way those disgustingly gorgeous women use blush, lip liner, and eye color, not so you look like them, but so you look like the best of yourself. Try a light foundation if your skin is uneven. Use a concealer if you have dark areas beneath your eyes as I have. If you can afford a session with a cosmetic specialist, do that. If not, have a small makeover at the local department store and treat yourself to a new product or two. It will do wonders for your morale and for your body image.

Men, I have a suggestion for you, too. Modernize your wardrobe a bit. Are you still wearing the tie-dyed shirts you wore in the seventies, or the wide-collared shirts that went with your leisure suits? Wander through a men's store at the local mall and see what men are wearing. Update yourself with a new shirt or a pair of slacks that really fit. Men's vanity amuses me. Many older men pride themselves that they wear the same size pants they wore twenty years ago. And they do. The waistline, however, is now substantially lower, their belts resting below their overhanging bellies. I don't care about the belly; it's the poorly fitting clothes that make a man look older.

Men, look at those long strands of hair that begin just over your ears and get combed up and over the top. You're really not fooling anyone. Bald may not be more beautiful than the luxurious head of hair you used to have, but it's not uglier, either. It just is. Ask Michael Jordan. Remember Telly Savalas and Yul Brynner? Consider returning those long locks to the side of your head where they belong.

Body image is much more about the way you feel about your good and bad points than about how you actually look. There was a story in the previous chapter about a man who bought his wife a lace bodysuit to try to fight her problems with body image. In the story that follows, Mark helped Gail learn a lesson about body image one evening by using a different sex toy.

GAIL AND MARK'S STORY

Gail was almost seventy and Mark was seventy-two. Their sex life had been very satisfying throughout their forty-three years of marriage. Recently, however, Mark had begun to suspect that Gail was avoiding the sexual side of their relationship. He wasn't horny all the time, the way he had been as a teenager, but he enjoyed sex with Gail and wasn't willing to give it up completely. He had tried to talk to his wife about it, but she staunchly denied that there was a problem.

For her part, Gail had begun to hate the sight she saw in the mirror in the bathroom after her shower each morning. Her skin had lost its elasticity and sagged in many places and her beauty marks had multiplied. Her breasts had lost the little uplift they had when she was younger and, as what seemed to her like the final insult, her pubic hair had almost disappeared. How could Mark look at her as a sexual being? How could he really be interested?

When Mark broached the subject of his disappearing sex life with his son Andy, the younger man said, "Hey, Dad, it's hard enough just imagining you and Mom having sex, much less you two doing it now that you're old. No offense, Dad."

"No offense, son."

Gail lightly touched on the subject of her disappearing sex life with their daughter. Liz had responded, "You know, sex is nice, but it's a strain, especially for Don and me, with the two kids and all. I think about how comfortable it must be for you now. You should be happy to slow down. Anyway, is all that sex stuff good for older people? You know, you're not kids anymore and Dad's heart isn't as healthy as it once was."

Gail sighed and changed the subject.

One afternoon, Mark decided that he would give one more try to reestablish the playful sexual relationship he and his wife had shared. He went to the video store and took out an XXX-rated video, one he remembered he and Gail had enjoyed several years earlier. That evening, sitting in the living room after the late news, Mark put the video in the tape player and pushed the button.

"What's that?" Gail asked.

"Its a video we both used to enjoy. Just be patient."

After the FBI warnings, a picture flashed on the screen of a woman walking through a misty landscape. "I think I remember this," Gail said. Then, as recognition dawned, her eyes widened. "It's that hot one about the couple who get trapped in the maze. The one with all the food. But why did you rent it now? We used to watch it, back when . . ."

"That's exactly why I rented it." He pulled the shoe box in which they kept their sex toys from under the sofa, where he had hidden it earlier.

"Where did you find that?" Gail asked. "We haven't used it for years."

"More's the pity."

"Come on, Mark, be real," Gail said over the rising music from the video. Parroting their daughter, she added, "We're not kids anymore."

"And what does that have to do with it? All the sex experts say there's no reason why we can't enjoy sex forever if we're so inclined. And I'm so inclined."

"But you've had one mild heart attack. . . ."

"And Dr. Shapiro says that exercise is good for me."

"Exercise?"

"I asked him about making love, and he's all for it. He told me it would do me good."

"You talked about our sex life with Dr. Shapiro?" Gail moaned. "I'll never be able to look at him again."

Mark put the box of toys on the coffee table and draped his arm around Gail's shoulders. "Be quiet and watch the movie."

On the screen, two lovers had become lost in an old-fashioned British hedgerow maze and were consoling each other with the knowledge that they would get out eventually. As they wandered, they came upon a clearing with a stone bench, several stone statues, a blanket, and a picnic basket. How those items got there was never explained in the film, but who really cared anyway? For several minutes, the two lovers fed each other goodies with their fingers; there were close-ups of them licking and sucking each other's fingers and lips and lots of sensual noises.

His eyes on the screen, Mark took a potato chip, dipped it into the low-fat sour cream and onion dip they had been eating, and fed it to Gail while they watched the lovers. Playing along, Gail did the same. Then Mark dipped his finger into the soft white goo and offered it to Gail.

Without thinking, Gail sucked her husband's fingers into her mouth and used her tongue to clean off every last bit of dip. When she realized what she had done, she said, "This is silly. It's for kids, not for people our age."

"Why not for people our age? I enjoyed that tremendously." Before Gail had time to respond, Mark spread some dip on her lips and licked it off. They kissed deeply, their arms wrapped around each other.

By the time their attention strayed back to the movie, the two screen lovers were naked, rolling around on the grass. Mark reached for Gail's T-shirt, but she resisted. "Why don't you want me to take your shirt off?" Mark asked.

"I just don't feel sexy," Gail responded. "I know I don't look sexy anymore." She turned her face away, but Mark grasped her chin and pulled her back to look at him.

"Then you don't think I look sexy anymore, either, I guess."

"Don't be ridiculous. Of course you're still sexy."

"But I'm no spring chicken." He stood up and turned sideways. "I've got a pot-belly, a few too many chins, and very little hair." He ran his hand over his bald pate.

"What does that matter?" Gail said. "I think you're sexy anyway."

"So why can't I think that you're sexy?"

"Because I look in a mirror and see what I see. I'm old."

"Okay. I'll give you that. You're old. So am I. So what?"

Mark noticed a small, slightly embarrassed smile on Gail's face. "But I don't feel sexy. I don't get wet and horny anymore," she said.

"And why do you think that is?"

"I don't know. Because I'm old."

"We've already established that. You didn't feel old twenty-five years ago, but for a while you didn't feel sexy then, either. Remember when the kids went off to college and you decided your life was over? You got over that quickly enough."

Gail remembered a trip to their cabin at the lake and a weekend of cavorting. "I did," she said, her eyes misty. "But that was just a hormonal phase I was going through."

"And now? Don't you think this might be a phase, too?" Mark sat back down and held his wife close. "I want to make playful, wonderful love with you. I still feel the same feelings, although I'll admit it takes longer to put any of them into action. Let's watch the movie and see what happens. Okay?"

Gail dropped her chin and stared at the TV. "Okay."

On the screen, the lovers had found a cucumber in the picnic basket and the man was slowly inserting it into his lover's vagina. "Oh God," Gail said, a bit breathless, "I'd forgotten that part."

Mark reached into the toy box and pulled out a slender dildo. "I hadn't. Maybe you just need to be reminded." In a flash, he had Gail's slacks off and had turned her body so she was stretched out on the sofa, her legs spread. As he had dozens of times before, Mark pulled a pair of scissors from the toy box and cut the sides of Gail's panties until he could pull the fabric away from her body.

"What are you doing?" Gail said, her voice half outrage and half amusement.

"That, my dear," Mark said, attempting to imitate a villain from the old Saturday-morning serials they used to watch at the movie theater, "would seem obvious." Mark took out a tube of lubricant and spread the slippery substance over the dildo. "Give up now. You want this and you know it, so don't fight it." Then he took a dollop of the lubricant and rubbed it slowly over Gail's vaginal tissues.

Gail squirmed. This was ridiculous. Wasn't it? Soon she realized that she really didn't want to fight it anymore. She did want to play. At their age, it was ridiculous, but she did want to "fool around," as they used to say.

Mark rubbed the cold, wet end of the toy against her flesh, then inserted it slowly and deeply into his wife's body. "Now, watch the movie."

Gail was getting hot. It seemed so unreal. She had convinced herself that she was beyond this part of life, but maybe she had been wrong. With her body delightfully filled, she watched the two lovers in the film. The man was sucking grapes from his lover's pussy.

"Remember the night I did that to you?" Mark asked, not expecting an answer. He pulled the dildo out, then pushed it in again. "Remember how that felt?"

She did remember, but it wasn't memories that were heating her body now. In and out the dildo slid, and she found her body getting hungry for more.

Now the screen lovers had a jar of jam and he was spreading the thick red paste over the woman's breasts, then licking it off. Mark left the dildo in place and pulled up Gail's T-shirt. Holding her breast in one hand, he kissed the nipple, watching it slowly become erect. "Yes, baby," he purred. "Oh yes."

Suddenly, Gail didn't feel old. She felt hot and hungry and ageless. She arched her back and pressed her hand against the nape of Mark's neck, holding his head against her.

Mark licked and sucked, frequently moving the dildo in Gail's body. Then he stood up and pulled down his pants and shorts. "I'm not as hard as I used to be," he said. "Will you let me love you anyway?"

Gail smiled and nodded. "I want you, you old fool," she said.

Mark took his semierect penis in his hand and, kneeling between Gail's spread legs, rubbed the tip over Gail's pussy. Then he pulled out the dildo and, still using his hand to guide his shaft, pushed into Gail's body. As he felt her heat, he reached between them and, in a familiar motion, rubbed her clit lightly as he thrust.

"Oh Mark," Gail said. "You feel wonderful."

After a long period of delicious thrusting and holding and stroking, Mark came first; then, as the lovers on the screen shifted position yet again, he stroked Gail's body until she climaxed, as well. Without moving, they watched the end of the film.

"That was wonderful," Mark said.

"And the film wasn't bad, either," Gail said, giggling.

"I've wanted this for so long. It was good, wasn't it?"

Gail heaved a large sigh. "It was terrific. It's difficult for me to adjust. I thought it was all over."

"You know, I can see us when we're each over one hundred, chasing each other around the porch of the retirement home. And every one else will be envious."

"With luck, everyone else will be doing the same thing."

Expectations. That's the biggest hurdle those of us over fifty face. We expect to be old. Our children expect us to be old. Society expects us to be old. Old and used up and "comfortable." Horse pucky. Although physical reactions change as we age, the pleasures that can be gained from sharing a satisfying sexual relationship remain unchanged. For most reasonably healthy older lovers, there are no activities that should be automatically excluded. All the games you used to play are still available. All the sexual goals you used to set are still achievable, with a few modifications. Just don't give up!

There are real sexual problems associated with aging, and I don't mean to minimize them. There are, however, benefits, as well.

First, let's talk about the postmenopausal woman.

After menopause, a woman no longer menstruates,

and she can't get pregnant; the production of female hormones slows, then stops. There is a distinct advantage to these changes—no more need for birth control. If you and your partner are strictly monogamous, throw out the diaphragm, the pills, the foam, and the condoms (although you may want to keep the condoms for other reasons, like anal sex). However, if you and your partner haven't been exclusive and monogamous for at least five years, continue to use condoms to prevent the spread of disease, and consult your doctor and have an AIDS test.

Until the age of thirty-eight, I had used the pill for birth control. Then, after my divorce and my re-entry into the land of the dating female, I used a diaphragm—AIDS hadn't been discovered yet. When my gynecologist confirmed that my hot flashes and irregular periods meant that I was going through menopause, I expected to be unhappy. Actually, I was thrilled.

Ed and I found each other when I was forty-two and he was forty-seven. By this time, since AIDS was a significant threat and both of us had previously been anything but monogamous, we used condoms. Finally, several years later, I was told that I could no longer conceive, and we had been monogamous for all that time. With glee, I threw out the diaphragm, put the condoms in a drawer for playtimes when we wanted to use them, and for the first time since before my marriage, I made love without the need to remember anything. A distinct advantage.

For me, in addition to the problems with body image that Gail and so many other women experience, the major downside of menopause was that my body didn't lubricate as well as it used to. In many women, this can cause intercourse to be painful. For me, it has a more important and, in my opinion, more insidious consequence. I didn't feel as though I was excited if I wasn't wet. I kept waiting, wondering whether I was going to feel "hot" between my legs ever again. That was my baggage, my problem.

I stumbled on an article in a magazine that discussed this, and my anxiety was somewhat relieved. The article said that women can become just as aroused after menopause as before, even though their vaginal tissues remain dry. The lack of lubrication is a physical thing, not a sexual one.

Then, more important, Ed and I had exciting sex a few times using a lubricant and I climaxed just as I had for years. Although my tissues were dry, my body was as excited as it had ever been. It took quite a while for me to smash down those shards of fear about "no good sex ever again." But I have, and Ed and I cavort as we always have and, I hope, always will.

A *warning:* There are many commercially available vaginal lubricants, from K-Y jelly to products you can buy from catalogs. They work well and even come in assorted flavors, which can also enhance oral sex. Use one of those products—*not* anything else—for vaginal lubrication. Vaseline, baby oil, mineral oil, and other types of petroleum-based products can clog pores and lead to vaginal irritation and infection. Also, these lubricants can break down the latex in a condom, causing a complete elimination of their usefulness as a disease barrier at just the wrong time.

A few years after being told I was not able to conceive anymore, I went to my gynecologist, and to relieve my hot flashes and help with my cholesterol problem, she suggested hormone-replacement thera-py. Now I take my pills every morning and my body lubricates the way it always did. But this is not what's making the sex better, by the way.

Taking synthetic female hormones is recommended by most doctors for most women, but it's not for every-one. In my case, it completely eliminated my awful hot flashes, and once my doctor and I found the proper dosage, I have all the advantages of natural hormones, but I no longer get my period. Ain't science grand!

Another subtle problem for the postmenopausal woman is that the clitoral hood, the tissue that covers the clitoris, becomes thinner as the years pass. This can mean that stimulation that used to be exciting is now irritating, almost painful. This thinning happens so slowly that many woman think it's always been that way and neglect to discuss the problem with their part-ners. Mentioning that a lighter touch would be more enjoyable can completely alleviate this difficulty.

For men, the problems of aging can be more subtle and, in some ways, even more insidious. An erect penis is an indication of manliness. A "limp dick" is a symbol of failure for a man. You're not a "stud" any-more, so you should be put out to pasture with the old horses who can't impregnate the young mares any longer. More horse pucky.

It is certainly true that for an older man, erections happen more slowly, aren't as firm, and don't last as long. It's not the end of everything, and it won't be unless you let it. It does mean that it may take a hand or even a mouth on the penis to get it sufficiently erect for penetration. Frankly, I don't see that as a draw-back, but a pleasure.

By the way, I've had enough lovers to make the following statement: For me, and I believe for most women, once a penis is inside my vagina, I could care less how big it was when it went in. My body easily accommodates to both larger and smaller men, and the physical sensation is really no different. The "hung like a horse" myth is just that. As a matter of fact, I was once with a man who was exceedingly "well hung." Unfortunately, he was a lousy lover and depended on his size to make up for a lack of communication and caring. And, a day later, I was so sore that I ended up at my doctor's. I never made love with him again.

Also, from the woman's point of view, once a man's penis is inside, she has no significant change in sensation because it is rock-hard or slightly softer. I can tell you that I particularly enjoy placing my partner's penis inside of me while it is still soft and then telling a story or using a few selected erotic images and feeling it get harder as he gets more excited. In this case, I can feel the change, and it's wonderful. Although the harder penis doesn't change my pleasure, it indicates my partner's arousal.

Slower erections in older men are an added benefit for those who once suffered from premature ejaculation. This problem is almost eliminated because of the physical changes due to aging. It takes longer for an older man to get sufficiently stimulated to ejaculate. This added time may give you and your partner an opportunity to enjoy some of the long make-out sessions that gave you problems earlier in your sexual life.

Men often find that they climax less often and that it takes longer from the height of sexual tension to orgasm. In addition, the time between erections also gets longer. When you were twenty, you could probably get a second erection within a few minutes of ejaculation. As the years passed, that refractory period got longer and longer. These timing shifts are a result of the physiological changes that happen with age. But most men assume that this time lag will get longer and longer, until climax just doesn't happen anymore. Or they worry that eventually they will not be able to "get it up." Still more horse pucky. As long as you're healthy, intercourse can and will still happen if you want it to, and ejaculations will occur naturally, when your body is ready.

Men, keep something in mind. One of the differences women bemoan is that men seem to get hot almost instantly, while women may take fifteen to thirty minutes to become fully aroused. Many women complain that they frequently aren't totally aroused by the time the man enters and climaxes. This becomes less and less of a problem as the years pass, since a man's timing and a woman's become more in sync.

If you are beginning to focus on that lengthening time span before intercourse, you are missing an entire segment of sexual enjoyment. It's the trip that's the pleasure, not the destination. Make a mental effort to enjoy the play, the eroticism of the journey you and your partner are taking through sexuality each time you make love, and try not to concentrate so completely on the orgasm at the other end. I find there are times that I don't climax, not because something goes wrong, but because there is so much pleasure in the experience itself that an orgasm isn't necessary.

Impotence due solely to age is infrequent in men. Let me say that again, louder. *Impotence due solely to age is infrequent in men.* However, there are other causes of lack of sexual function.

A frequent cause of temporary impotence is medication. Many doctors don't inform patients that cardiac drugs, for example, can inhibit a man's penis from becoming erect. Unfortunately, too often the patient is so embarrassed by his impotence that he doesn't mention it on future visits. Men, talk to your doctor. He or she may be able to adjust your medication to minimize or completely eliminate this problem. I know it's difficult, but isn't a lifetime of continued good sex worth a few minutes of awkwardness?

A suggestion: Since levels of testosterone (the male hormone) are at their highest in the morning, it may make erection and ejaculation easier. Have a quick cup of coffee, if you must, and then go back to bed. Making love in the daylight can be very enjoyable, particularly for those who have always made love at night, in the dark. Try having her lie in the bed with her naked pussy in a shaft of warm sun. That's an area of a woman's body that may never have felt anything like that before. It's truly delicious—and I speak from experience.

Diseases can also play havoc with erections, either temporarily or permanently. If your impotence is a permanent result of an uncorrectable condition, there are other strategies that can be used to allow you to continue to satisfy both your partner and, more importantly, yourself. Talk to your doctor, or consult a specialist on male reproductive function. From implants to drugs, there are more and more products entering the market every year. And they work.

For both sexes, changes in nerve and circulatory function alter the way things feel on our bodies. For many aging partners, areas that used to be erogenous are no longer special. Sensations seem to be numbed. I find that, due to decades of bras and a decrease in blood flow, my nipples are less sensitive and become erect far more slowly. These changes in both men and women are often misinterpreted, overlooked, or ignored, allowing them eventually to dominate the relationship.

Some suggestions: Since sexual patterns so thoroughly ingrained are difficult to break, try something as simple as swapping sides of the bed. It gives things a whole new perspective. Or try a hand or foot massage or a long session brushing your partner's hair. These simple sensual pleasures are often overlooked and can lend a new depth of feeling to a relationship.

Maybe now is the time to map your partner's body. Place your partner out on the bed, naked, and begin with a light massage. A light stroking massage can be done without messy oils or creams. Check the backs of knees, insides of ankles, and elbows. Try the nape of the neck or the skin just behind the ear. Find the ticklish places and caress them if your partner likes, or avoid them entirely. I, for one, hate to be tickled. Touch all over and make new mental notes of what causes your partner to shiver or moan, and what places are no longer as sensitive as they used to be.

Once you know his or her body, try some different sensations, a feather, a leaf, a cotton ball, a furry glove, a rose petal, or a piece of silk. Then switch to a piece of rough fabric or even fine sandpaper. Try a bag filled with warm water or an ice cube. Try the lightest touch of your finger or a scratch with a fingernail. Try everything and use the information for future lovemaking sessions. Then turn your partner over and begin again.

● ● ●

An old bull and a young bull stood on a hill overlooking a herd of cows. "Let's run down the hill and fuck a cow," the young bull said.

The old bull sighed. "Let's walk *down the hill,"* he said, *"and fuck them all."*

TRY SOMETHING NEW:
STORYTELLING

Reading erotica aloud can be a wonderful way to begin an evening. Hearing about the exploits of others indulging their every sexual whim can lead to new heights of sensual play. As you already know, there are dozens of stories in this book that you can read to your partner, or ask him or her to read to you. Since some people have difficulty saying specific words or discussing explicit sex, you can "force" or "dare" your partner to read aloud. You may be most pleasantly surprised by the results.

Telling stories in the dark is a variation, another delicious prelude to lovemaking. Creating erotic situations and "what if" scenarios allows you to delve into realms forbidden in ordinary activity. You can be in absolute control, or totally give up control. You can make love with an audience, in the weightlessness of space, in a hot tub or a snowbank. Anything's possible.

You can also talk about activities that you've always dreamt about, and if your partner's radar is functioning, maybe he or she will hear your request for a new, off-center activity.

You can always make up your own story, of course, but in case you're not feeling creative, I've included some story starters, setups of familiar themes that you can use to begin your midnight tale of erotic pleasure. And, of course, you can lead these stories into areas that you want to explore. Be very aware of your partner's reaction to a new sexual situation. You may be surprised at what's dwelling in the dark recesses of his or her fantasy world. You can help to bring those fantasies into the light and maybe make some of them come true.

So here are some stories. I'll start them and you and your loved one can finish them.

The Detective

"So you need me to find your stolen jewels before your son-in-law finds out they're missing," the tall, lean, casually dressed man in his mid-fifties said. "Have I got that right so far?"

"Yes, Mr. Cooper," Meredith said. "I must have them back before the family party this weekend." Behind her back, she crossed her fingers in an unconscious gesture. There was so much at stake, and Cooper had come well recommended. She had found out that he had done work for her company before. This, however, was personal.

"And how much are you prepared to pay me?" The detective lounged behind his desk, his easygoing manner in direct contrast to the sexual charge he was sending out.

"I'll pay you a thousand dollars now and another thousand when you find the jewels. That's everything I can spare." She had to convince him to help. He was her last hope.

"What about the jewels? They must be worth a fortune."

"They are, but they're not mine. They were part of my mother's estate, left in my care but in trust for my daughter. My son-in-law is threatening to take me to court if I don't hand them over. It's not the court that bothers me, but he also says he won't let me see my grandchildren, and my daughter will go along with him."

"I gather you don't like him much."

"Let's just say that he's not my favorite person. And I don't really trust him, either."

"I see. You think there's something else going on here?"

"Yes." Meredith sighed and tried to relax her gritted teeth. "He saw me wearing them at a formal business dinner we attended together recently. He's a vice president of my late husband's firm. I spent the night in the hotel after the dinner and now the necklace, bracelet, and ring are gone."

"Well, well, well," Cooper said. "It seems you are in a bit of trouble." He opened the bottom drawer of his desk and indolently propped his feet on top. "Two thousand doesn't really seem enough to compensate me for my trouble."

Meredith shifted in the uncomfortable chair and rubbed the palms of her hands down her tailored black slacks. She stared at her knees, then gazed back at the attractive man. He had made himself quite clear and she had nowhere else to go. "I might be able to go to three thousand. I'm not a wealthy woman, Mr. Cooper."

He didn't move, just raised an eyebrow.

She sighed and stood up. "I'm sorry I bothered you."

"Don't be in such a hurry to leave," Cooper said, his eyes roaming her shapely body. "Maybe we can make other arrangements."

Meredith slowly lowered herself back into the chair and raked her long fingers through her short, curly salt-and-pepper hair. "Like?" She had a feeling she knew exactly what he was referring to, but she would wait and hear it from his sensual mouth.

"Like *you.* You're a very sexy lady and I find that you excite me. I'll forgo my fee and find your jewels if you agree to spend a weekend with me when this is all over. I won't force you into my bed, although that's where you'll end up, I hope. I just want enough time to convince you that you and I can make your body sing with pleasure, the likes of which you've never experienced before."

Meredith took a deep, shuddering breath. Cooper was gazing at her with piercing blue eyes that seemed to see into her soul. She felt wetness begin between her legs and her nipples tingled. She looked at his sandy blond hair and wondered how it would feel between her fingers. She stared at his brushy mustache and could almost feel it scraping her breasts. She took another deep breath and nodded. "All right, I agree," she whispered. "I agree."

The Telepath

"I can see that you're new here," the man said, taking the seat next to Serena in the shuttle station.

"Yes, I am," Serena said. "I'm waiting for the dispatcher to get me a flitter-car to take me to my hotel."

"Have you ever been off-world before?" the man asked.

"No," Serena said, breathless with the excitement of new adventure. "This is my first trip. I've saved for months to get here. I have wanted to visit Panar since I came of age." She took in the man's slightly greenish skin and sixth finger. "You're a Panaran," she said, awed.

The man smiled. "Rolt is my name, and yes, I'm a Panaran. And you're Terran."

"My name's Serena." She extended her hand. "It's very nice to meet you."

Rather than taking her hand, the man said, "How much do you know about Panarans, and particularly those of the Russss class?" The word hissed from his mouth softly, like the sound of a beautiful but terribly dangerous snake.

Serena snatched her hand back. "I'm so sorry. I didn't realize you were Russss. You're a telepath."

"Only by touch." He fixed her with his eyes. "But if I was to touch you, I would know every thought, every desire. It makes us very useful as business nego-tiators, and as lovers."

Serena blushed to the roots of her hair. She had read about these Russss classers and the stories had drawn her to this planet like a magnet. She hadn't expected to meet one so quickly, however. "That's very interesting," she said, hands trembling.

"I don't have to be a telepath to know it's much more than interesting to you. I have my personal flitter-car outside. I could buy you a drink and you could learn a bit more about Russss classers like me."

She was more tempted than she had ever been. She was experienced in love, as everyone was expected to be in this day and age, but there were so many erotic pleasures she longed to experience. And Russss classers were the most skilled of lovers.

"Your flitter-car, Miss," the dispatcher said, lights on his panel blinking. "May I take your luggage?"

Rolt extended his hand toward her. "Should he take your luggage, or should I?"

Serena gazed into Rolt's fathomless almost-black eyes. She reached out and touched his hand lightly. She turned to the dispatcher. "Thank you," she said, "but I won't be needing that flitter-car after all." She tightened her grip on Rolt's hand and together they walked toward his flitter-car.

The Next-Door Neighbor

"Well, Adam," Lisa said, "it's good to see you back for the summer."

"It's good to be back," Adam said, admiring the way his next-door neighbor seemed to get more beautiful each year. Although she was at least forty, she had been the center of his most graphic sexual fantasies for most of his teenaged years.

Adam watched Lisa's eyes roam over his body. He straightened his back and was suddenly glad he had spent all those hours in the weight room at college. He also realized that he had selected the particularly becoming light blue polo shirt and white shorts because he thought he might be seeing her today.

"How did your junior year go?" she asked, sitting back down on her lawn chair, her long, shapely legs stretched out enticingly.

Her one-piece bathing suit both concealed and

revealed, and Adam swallowed hard as he imagined the breasts and belly and velvety flesh beneath. "It went well," Adam said, swinging his tennis racket. "Got my overall grade point average up to a three point one."

"That's wonderful," Lisa said. "The best I ever did was two point five."

"I'm sure you did just fine," Adam said, desperately wanting to continue the conversation but unable to think of anything more to say. He watched Lisa shift her position, revealing more of the soft skin on the inside of her thigh.

"Any girlfriends?" Lisa asked.

"A few." But no one like you, he wanted to say.

"Umm, I'll bet. A gorgeous guy like you must have dozens. I'll bet your Saturday nights are works of art."

Works of art indeed, Adam thought. If she only knew that his Saturday nights usually consisted of little more than frustration. A sexual flop, that's what he was.

"Adam?" Lisa said after a long silence. "Come here." She tapped the chair next to her.

Adam put his tennis racket down, crossed the floral border between the two back lawns, and sat in the chair she had indicated.

"Tell me. Aren't those college girls good enough for you? Don't they make you happy?" She placed her warm palm on his bare thigh. "Don't they give you what you want?" Ever so slowly, she moved her hand higher up his thigh.

Adam stared at the hand, and the contrast between her long red nails and the light tan of his skin. "S-s-sometimes," he stammered.

"But not always?" The hand moved down again, the fingernails brushing the inside of his thigh.

"Not always," he managed to say.

The hand moved upward again, closer to the painful erection he was trying unsuccessfully to hide. "Sometimes you want something more, right? Someone more experienced, a woman who can give you all that you're entitled to."

"Sometimes."

"You know, of course, that you're a very attractive boy. No, make that man now." The hand squeezed his upper thigh. "Oh yes, definitely a man now." Her index finger brushed his hard penis. "A man whom I've been watching for years."

"Watching?" Adam could barely breathe.

"Oh yes. I've been watching you grow and mature. And I've been wondering about you, too. Whether you were happy. Whether you were learning all the things they teach at college. Whether you were engaging in the right extracurricular activities." The hand squeezed and her knuckle massaged his shaft. "There's so much to learn."

He swallowed again. "Yes, there is."

"I can help you if there are any courses you're having trouble with." Somehow, she maneuvered his zipper down about an inch and her finger insinuated its way inside. Now she was rubbing his cock through only the soft fabric of his undershorts. "We could go inside and study together right now, if you like. Everyone's away for the weekend and we would have no distractions from our lessons."

"We could do that, I guess."

She withdrew her finger, then took his hand. She stood and pulled him up beside her. "So tall. Have I told you I like tall men?"

Adam took her hand and they walked through the back door and into the darkened playroom.

The Secret Formula

Joel knew that the secret of his company's newly developed high-powered explosive was finally in good hands. So far, three people were dead and one was in the hospital in a coma as a result of trying to protect the information from those who would misuse it. He had suspected several times that he was being followed, but now, in his hotel room near the airport, he felt relatively safe. He had stashed the folder with the complex formulas in a carefully selected place. Just before flight time, he would retrieve it. And in less than a day, it would be safely at the lab.

He heard the knock at the door and reached for his handgun. "Yes?" he called, the gun ready should he need it.

"The company sent me." The voice was soft and melodious—a woman in her twenties, he suspected. No trace of an accent, but she had to be up to no good. His company had told him nothing about sending anyone for him.

"What company?" he called.

"Listen," the voice said, "I don't want to yell all this through the door. Who knows who might be listening?"

Joel made his way across the room and looked through the peephole. The woman was a knockout: long red hair that curled over her bosom, green eyes, and clear white skin. She held up a picture ID card so he could see it through the tiny opening. It looked genuine, but he knew it couldn't be. A very good forgery maybe. He knew everyone at the company, but he didn't know her. "The bad guys must know me well," he muttered, a reluctant smile spreading across his face. "God, I love that colleen look." He reached for the doorknob and turned it.

"You certainly took your time," the woman said, stalking into the room on long, shapely legs. Her skirt was short and tight, her blouse loose and sexy.

As Joel closed the door, he could feel his body react. He really didn't have time for this. "Okay, you're in," he snapped. "What do you want?"

"My name's Maureen and I'm supposed to go to the States with you." She pulled a plane ticket from her purse and showed it to Joel.

The ticket was for the same flight, and, if he remembered his seat assignment correctly, she would be sitting next to him. "Why?"

"The company thought you'd be less conspicuous if we traveled as a tourist couple returning from our wedding trip."

"Really?" he said, his eyebrow raised in disbelief.

"Really." She looked at his expression, then continued. "Look, this wasn't my idea. I just joined this ridiculous company three weeks ago and suddenly they shove a ticket in my face and give me this cock-and-bull story. I have no idea who the hell you are, or why you're here, for that matter."

"Really," he said again. "Three weeks. That's a good story. It covers why I don't know you." He lifted one bright red lock of hair from her chest and rubbed it between his fingers. "And I wouldn't have forgotten you. You can be sure of that."

He watched Maureen tremble. "Look, I'm new at this and I want this job very badly," she said, her voice quavering as Joel's knuckles grazed her breast. "But I don't think . . ."

"You don't think what?" He grinned and released her hair.

She took a quavering breath. "Let's just try to make the best of this till flight time." She crossed the room and sat on the only chair in the small room.

"Sure," Joel said, settling on the bed opposite her, "we can do that. But the flight's not until tomorrow, and we have all of tonight to kill." His eyes roamed her body as she shifted position. He watched her take another deep breath, which forced her breasts against the soft fabric of her blouse. "Anyway, isn't that your job?"

"I don't understand."

"I don't believe a word of that ridiculous story you just handed me. I think you want some information from me and you'll do anything to get it."

She gave him a "who me?" look and said, "That's crazy."

"Whether it is or not, we have to spend the night together in this room while you try to convince me that you work for the company, or whatever your assignment is. I won't tell you anything, but you can try." He reached out and stroked her breast with the palm of his hand. "You can use any means you like."

Suddenly, Maureen laughed. "You're just like they said you'd be, a flirt and a lecher. You really think we'll spend the night in your bed."

Joel cocked his head to one side and again looked Maureen over. Instead of replying, he grinned, a grin that had usually gotten him anything he wanted.

"Well," Maureen said, crossing her long legs, "we'll see, won't we?"

The Returning Hero

Annie hadn't seen Evan Chambers since high school. He had been the toughest kid in school, and due to a few scrapes with the law, he had been given the option of joining the military after graduation or going to jail. The Monday after commencement, he had swaggered through town in his fatigues, saying good-bye to all his friends. She had watched from the top of the library steps.

Now, almost twenty years later, Evan was back, a colonel in the army and a real hero. During a training exercise, something had gone wrong with a test missile, and it was Evan's quick thinking that saved several men from death. There had been long articles about his heroics week after week in the local paper and, hungering for more details, she had read every one several times.

Annie now sat in the local diner, nibbling at her chicken potpie, gazing at Evan's picture on the front page of the local paper. LOCAL HERO MAKES GOOD AND RETURNS TO BIRTHPLACE. She gazed at the picture. He looked so handsome in his uniform, silver at his temples. Suddenly, a ripple went through the crowd. She looked up, and there he was, tall, clean-shaven. It was as though she had just seen him a few days before. He was just as gorgeous as she had thought he was in their senior year, but different—much more mature.

"Evan Chambers," a booming voice said, "good to see you back."

"Good to be back, Mr. Willoughby."

"How long has it been?"

"Almost twenty years."

"Twenty years," Mr. Willoughby mumbled. Then the

man lifted his three-hundred-pound frame from a small chair and walked over to Evan. "Are you back to stay or just passing through?" He draped his arm around the uniformed man's shoulders.

"I'm not really sure yet," Evan said, his voice deep and exciting. "I'm thinking of retiring from the military, but I'm not sure what I want to do yet."

Annie felt her heart pound in her chest. Evan was looking around the small diner, trying to find a place to sit, and attempting to move out from under Mr. Willoughby's beefy arm. Since it was the height of the dinner hour, Annie knew that there were no empty tables.

"Full up, isn't it?" Mr. Willoughby said. "Well, boy, why don't you join the wife and me?"

"Just a moment," Evan said, crossing the room and heading toward Annie's table, his back to the Willoughbys. He placed the palms of his hands on her table and leaned toward her. Under his breath, he said, "I don't think we've met, but save me. I can't stand that loud-mouth. Let me sit with you. Please."

Annie smiled. She could refuse him nothing. "Of course, Evan. Join me if you like."

Without letting anyone else overhear, he whispered, "What's your name?"

"Annie."

"Hey, Mr. Willoughby, I'm sure you'll understand if I eat with Annie."

"Sure, Colonel," Mr. Willoughby boomed. "I'd eat with a lovely thing like that if I could, too. Just be nice to her, you heartbreaker. She's only been divorced for two years."

"Harvey," Mrs. Willoughby yelled. "Leave those two alone and sit back down and feed your face."

"Yes, Celia."

As Mr. Willoughby returned to his table, Evan leaned forward. "Gee, thanks, Annie."

His grin was infectious, and Annie found herself smiling, too. "It's nothing. It's so good to see you back, and a colonel at that."

"You know, you look familiar. Do we know each other?"

"Have I changed that much? I'm Annie Flynn. It was Annie McGovern. From high school. We were in Mr. Cabbott's homeroom together, senior year." Annie knew from his gaze that he thought she had changed a lot—for the better, she hoped.

Evan's eyes widened as he gazed at the woman who sat across from him. "Annie McGovern? Long straight hair and braces?"

"Yup. That was me." She was suddenly glad she had worn her best teal blue dress. She played with her fork as he looked her over, obviously liking what he saw. "You've changed, too."

The waitress arrived at the table. "Welcome back, Colonel Chambers."

"Thanks. I'd just like what she's having," he said, motioning toward Annie's potpie.

"Coming up," the waitress said.

Evan's appreciative gaze returned to the woman across the table. "Annie McGovern. You're divorced, Mr. Willoughby said. I can't believe someone let you get away. Wow. Listen, let's finish dinner and go out dancing. We can catch up on old times and such. Does the old Melrose Inn still have dancing on Saturday nights?"

As he spoke, his knee brushed hers beneath the table. "I really should get home," Annie said.

Evan reached across the table and took her hand.

"Please. I've just gotten here, and I'd like to sit with you so we can get to know each other much better." As he stared directly into Annie's eyes, she felt heat building in her belly.

"Well, the inn does still have music."

He winked, the danger obvious in the way he rubbed her knee with his. Clearly, there was still some of the bad boy left in him. "Good. I'd really like to be with you."

Unable or unwilling to resist, Annie whispered, "Yes."

The First Visit

Kevin walked through the ordinary-looking doors of the four-story brownstone and looked around. He was astonished. It looked like an ordinary hallway, with a small mahogany table holding a crystal vase filled with fresh flowers. He walked forward, into what he assumed was the living room. The tremendous room was tastefully decorated in an eclectic mélange of overstuffed chairs, side tables, standing lamps, and two cream-colored leather sofas. Several couples and a few individual women sat talking quietly, drinks in hand.

"Good evening," a voice said from behind him.

Kevin turned and gazed at the beautifully dressed woman who stood there, her right hand extended toward him. The woman was a knockout: tall, slender, and perfectly made-up, with huge brown eyes and carefully cut medium brown hair that fell to just below the line of her jaw. She was dressed in a soft wool suit in a muted raspberry, with a gray silk blouse beneath.

"Good evening," he said when he realized he'd been staring. He took her hand and marveled at her strong, sure grip.

"You must be Kevin," she said. "I'm Heather, and I'm not what you expected, am I?"

Kevin tried not to be rude, but he found himself tongue-tied, unable to respond at all.

"It's all right," Heather said. "I'm not what anyone expects. I gather you're from California?"

"Yes," Kevin managed to mumble.

"Well, Mark Cantor recommended you without reservation, and any friend of Mark's is, of course, a friend of mine. Welcome."

"Thank you," Kevin said softly. He had no clue as to what to do or say next.

"You know what we do here. We're kind of a dating service. Cantor Enterprises has a standing account with us, so there's no problem on that score. We're having a sort of party tonight. Would you like a drink?"

"Sure. Gin and tonic?"

"Right away." The woman walked toward one corner of the large room, where a white-jacketed man was making drinks.

Kevin tried to keep his jaw from hanging open. When Mark had suggested that he take a night off from the meetings they had been attending all week, Kevin had readily agreed. It had taken more convincing, however, before he agreed to visit what Mark had described as "the most amazing escort service in New York."

Mark had continued, "It has to be seen to be believed, that I can assure you."

Kevin had finally been convinced, but he hadn't expected anything like this.

"You expected something like the Chicken Ranch,"

Heather said, returning from the bar with Kevin's drink. "From *Best Little Whorehouse*."

Kevin looked at her ruefully. "I guess I did," he said.

"We're not like that at all," Heather said, leading Kevin to one of the leather sofas. "We're here to fill a need that many lonely men from out of town have. We have women of all kinds to suit all interests. You can take one of them out to dinner and see what develops, or you can sit here and talk to several women before you decide. You can go upstairs to one of our suites of rooms for however long you like, or you can leave and come back another time. You can even entertain several women, if that's your interest, or one or more men. We're very low-key, very friendly, and very accommodating."

Heather discussed the house rules about condoms and explained that many of the girls had a specialty. "Is there any fantasy you've always had but never had a chance to explore?"

Kevin felt Heather's hand rest on his knee. His mind raced. Fantasy? There were so many things he had read about in magazines. He looked around the room at the gorgeous women, any one of whom was his for the asking.

"Well," he said, "there is one thing I'd like."

AGELESS FANTASIES

Get out your bookmark, because here are the last three ageless fantasies.

MELISSA'S FANTASY

It had been a long, hard day at the office, and Melissa was glad it was over. All day, the air conditioning in the building had been switching on and off, mostly off, and by late afternoon, her office was like a sauna. She couldn't wait to get home and strip off her hot, sweaty clothes. God, I'd strip naked right here if I thought I could get away with it, she thought as she stood waiting for the elevator.

Three other people stood at the closed elevator doors, all looking as rumpled as she knew she did. As she glanced to her left, she saw the cute new guy from Accounting. He had black hair and blue eyes and was tall and well built. "Terrible day," she said to him.

"Oh yeah," he said. "I thought I'd melt."

"I'm Melissa. From Shipping."

"Doug." He looked at his watch, then at the elevator indicator, having already dismissed her.

Melissa sighed as the elevator doors slid open and she entered. As the express elevator dropped from the twenty-fourth floor, she turned and wiggled into the small amount of space between Doug and the closed doors. She could feel his briefcase pressing against the backs of her thighs. She closed her eyes.

Suddenly, halfway between 21 and 20, there was a clunking sound and a bump. Then the lights went out and everything stopped.

"Hey, what's this?" a man's gravelly voice said.

"Shit," a woman responded. "This is all I need. No air conditioning, now this."

"Damn," a younger woman said, "I can't see a thing.

Aren't there supposed to be emergency lights in this car?"

Bodies were moving around, rearranging themselves to make use of the little space available. "I'll find the alarm," Gravel Voice said.

A moment later, the harsh clang of the alarm bell jangled everyone's already-raw nerves. "Shit," a woman said. "Stop that noise. I've already got a headache."

Melissa instinctively moved slightly away from the sound and felt her back press against a man's chest, a man she assumed was Doug. "Sorry," she whispered.

The man pressed his crotch against Melissa's back and she became very aware of the ridge of flesh beneath his tailored slacks. Being a tall woman, Melissa knew her bottom was just the proper height to cradle the hardness. I should move, she thought. Move forward, against the door. Stop this erotic invasion of my space. But rather than move forward, she pressed backward ever so slightly. God, it feels so good.

Suddenly, she became aware of a hand sliding around her waist at the junction of her summer silk blouse and soft flowing skirt. Slowly, the hand slipped up her ribs to cup her breast. She wanted to move away, without embarrassing anyone, of course. But she didn't. No one could see a thing in the pitch-darkness. The hand kept moving, kneading and pinching her breast. She wanted to resist, but instead, she let her head fall back against the shoulder behind her, her arms limp at her sides.

"How long do you think we'll be stuck here?" a younger man's voice asked.

"Lord only knows," another man answered.

Melissa felt a mouth on her ear, breathing hot air

into the opening, then nipping at the lobe. What if the lights come on? she wondered. Oh well, she could just stand up and no one would know anything. No one would know that his hand was making her pussy wet, making her hips grind against the hard cock that was cuddled in the crack of her bottom.

"Hey," the younger woman yelled, causing Melissa to straighten up. "Someone needs to get us out of here."

The hand began to unbutton her top, button by agonizing button. She wanted that hand on her hot flesh. But what if the lights came on? What if . . .

"Hello in the elevator," a distant voice cried.

"We're here," several passengers yelled.

"Get us out of here," other voices called.

By now, all the buttons of Melissa's blouse were open and the hand had lifted one breast from the cup of her demibra. Then the other breast was free and the hand was pulling and pinching the tender tips. She was unable to keep her hips still, and as she rubbed against the man behind her, she could feel his cock get bigger and harder.

"Brownout, folks," the distant voice said, then laughed.

"Hey, this isn't funny to us," Gravel Voice said. "It's hot as Hades in here and dark as the inside of a cat."

Melissa felt the man's other hand press the middle of her back. She leaned forward until her bare nipples contacted the cold steel of the elevator doors. As she started to pull back, a voice whispered in her ear, "Feel it."

She did. Her pussy was on fire as the cold tightened her already-erect nipples. The hand. Yes, the hand was moving downward. For a moment, it lay splayed across her belly, then moved lower still. The fingers pulled at the thin fabric of her skirt, raising it until they contacted the warm, wet skin of her thighs. She reached between her legs and tried to drag the hand to the spot where she needed to feel him.

"It will be another few minutes, folks," the outside voice yelled. "We're rerouting power to the elevator systems."

"God," the younger woman's voice said, "I don't know how much longer I can take this. I'm claustrophobic."

The man behind her said, "Be patient." Melissa felt the words rumble in his chest as he pressed the entire length of his body against hers. Was that comment for the woman or for her? She let her hand drop.

The man's fingers found the crotch of her panties and the small erect nub that was the center of all her thoughts now. He stroked around her outer lips, not quite touching her clit. "Patience," he whispered in her ear.

Then he found her and rubbed—back and forth with long strokes, then hard and fast, driving her higher and higher. Her breasts were like ice, her pussy on fire. What would happen if she came? she wondered. Usually very vocal, could she climax without crying out? And the man's cock was rubbing her backside faster and faster now. What would happen if he came? His clothes? Oh God, she didn't care. She reached for her orgasm.

"Just another minute," the outside voice said, and the car lurched a bit.

"Yes," one voice yelled.

"All right," another cried.

Drenched in sweat, Melissa came hard and hot, bit-ing the inside of her lip to keep silent. She felt the man come, too, bucking his hips against her backside. Oh God, she cried inside her mind. Oh God.

"Hey, lady," someone said. "Are you getting off?"

Melissa came back to reality. The elevator doors were open in front of her and several of the passengers had already wiggled out around her. "Sorry," she mumbled, still disoriented and incredibly excited by her daydream.

"Don't be sorry," the man behind her said. "Just take your time. It's too hot for rushing."

She turned and looked into Doug's sky blue eyes. "Thanks." She stepped from the elevator into the cool of the lobby.

"Hey. Melissa, isn't it? I'm really parched after that time in the elevator. How about stopping for a drink? Got a few minutes?"

"Gee, Doug," she said. "Yeah, I've got time. I'd like that."

DAVE'S FANTASY

Dave had been shopping in this particular mall bookstore for several years. It was convenient—since he worked just across the street—had a pretty good selection, and was a nice place to escape to during his lunch hour. He had gotten to know the staff pretty well, so he was surprised to see the new face behind the counter. Sherry, her name tag said. As he walked to the back of the store, he wondered what about this particular woman had given him a tight feeling in his shorts. As he analyzed the situation, he realized that she had looked him directly in the eye with a no-nonsense stare. Then her eyes had roamed his body, and when he had caught her looking at his crotch, there was a challenge in the way she returned his gaze.

As he stood in the erotica section, he imagined her making him do things.

She walked toward him. Quickly, he picked up a book and began looking through it, trying to look nonchalant. Too late, he realized he was holding *Female Dominance in a Man's World.*

She stopped beside him and glanced at the cover of the book. "I like that particular work," she said, "and I've read it many times." She raised an eyebrow. "Are you familiar with that form of sexuality?"

Standing this close, he could smell her perfume (Obsession?) and see deep into her light blue eyes. Unconsciously, his dick started to stiffen in his pants. She was spectacular, tall and lithe, with slender hands and long fingers with tapering bright red nails.

Before he could answer, she was looking over the shelves. "Have you read *Exit to Eden?* That's got some good scenes of dominance. It's a shame that so few people understand the need to be submissive. Ah, here it is." Bending from the waist to reach it, her back to Dave, he was treated to a perfect view of her tight little ass. Briefly, he saw just a hint of panties. They were black and very tight.

The bulge in his pants was unmistakable now. He hoped she wouldn't notice. "Yes. This is it. This book really turns me on." She handed it to Dave, and as he reached out to take it from her, she grasped his hand and squeezed it between her fingers and the book's unyielding cover.

Looking down, Dave saw her beautiful breasts and noticed her nipples hardening. His dick was so hard now, he really wanted to stroke it, but of course he couldn't. He felt flushed, and he knew his face was turning red. He wanted to look at her face, but somehow he couldn't. He kept his eyes on the floor, his hand unmoving in her grasp.

Her gaze fell onto the huge bulge in his pants and a mischievous smile crossed her lips. "I see that book does it for you, too," she said, her voice suddenly deep and throaty. "Come with me." She started to walk toward the back of the store, and when Dave remained immobile, she turned back. "I told you to do something."

Dave put his books on an empty shelf and followed this gorgeous creature. Opening the door marked EMPLOYEES ONLY, Sherry addressed the only other person back there. "Tom, watch the front for me."

"You bet," Tom said, leaving the room and walking up front.

Locking the door from the inside, Sherry pushed Dave against a worktable. "Now," she said, grabbing the bulge in the front of his trousers, "you seem to have a big secret in there." Sherry started rubbing his cock, practiced fingers quickly making him tremble.

Dave was speechless. He was about ready to grab her and rip her clothes off, when she suddenly patted his crotch and took a step back.

"I've been horny all day," Sherry said. "I need a good orgasm, and I have the feeling you're the right man for the job." While she spoke, she massaged her round, ripe breasts. "Just watch. When I'm ready, I'll tell you what I want you to do." She unbuttoned her blouse and threw it to one side, revealing a black lace bra, which was having trouble containing her massive breasts. While Dave watched, she unhooked the latch in the front and the bra fell to the floor.

Dave's breath caught in his throat as he saw the most perfect pair of breasts he had ever seen, with erect dark nipples that begged to be sucked. Without realizing it, Dave's hand started rubbing his erect cock.

The stinging slap on his wrist came so swiftly that Dave dropped his hands to his sides and stared at the floor. "I'm sorry."

"You bet you are," Sherry snapped. "I thought you understood. My pleasure is the only thing that matters here." She paused, then added, "Of course, if you're really good, I might let you come, too."

"Th-thank you," Dave stammered. His pulse was pounding and his entire body was shaking with excitement.

"That's better," Sherry said sweetly. "I think we understand each other."

As Dave watched, Sherry turned and, bending over slightly, unbuttoned and unzipped her short, close-fitting black skirt and pushed it down to the ground. Dave got a look at her skintight black lace panties. The garment was laced up the center of the front with a red satin ribbon.

"Come over here and kneel in front of me!" Dave knew she would brook no resistance, and he had none. He was hers and he would do whatever she wanted.

Dave knelt. He was only inches away from the pussy of this incredible goddess, and he could smell her musky scent. He wanted her. More than he had ever wanted anything, he wanted this woman.

"Take my panties off," she commanded, "using only your teeth."

Dave's pulse started to race. Gripping the top of one end of the bright red ribbon in his teeth, he tugged. The knot came undone and, as he pulled, the sides parted. His nose brushed against her silky pubic hair, causing Sherry to let out a little gasp. Dave continued working on pulling the panties down until her pussy was totally exposed. He was unsure of what to do next, so he sat back on his haunches and waited.

"You're well trained," she said. "Have you had women like this before?"

"No. You are the first woman who understood."

"Understood what? Tell me exactly." When he hesitated, she snapped, "I gave you an instruction."

"You understand what I want. To be told. To serve you."

Sherry grinned. "You're right. I do understand. Do you want to touch me?"

"Oh yes," Dave groaned.

"So sweet," she said, ruffling his hair, "and you may serve me, give me pleasure.

"Thank you," he whispered. His hands moved around behind her and stroked her fine firm ass while he pulled her closer to him, as close as she could be. Using his tongue and lips, he licked and kissed all around her pussy and thighs. Sherry's gasps came faster and faster, soon turning to sighs, then to moans.

"Very good," she said. "You have a very talented mouth. I want your tongue to get me off. Now!"

Dave found Sherry's protruding clit with his tongue and licked it. Sherry's knees buckled with the sensation, forcing her to grab Dave's head for support. Not missing a beat, Dave kept licking and sucking, finding her slit and fucking it with his tongue.

Sherry started bucking her hips, offering her pussy and forcing his tongue deeper and deeper.

"I can pleasure you in other ways," Dave said. "May I? Please?"

"Yes," she hissed.

Dave wet his index finger with her slick pussy juices and tickled Sherry's tender asshole with it. When he pushed it inside, she exploded in orgasm. "Don't stop," she cried, so Dave continued rubbing her asshole and licking her cunt.

After a few moments, Sherry pushed Dave back onto his haunches. "That was very good indeed." She stood, magnificently naked, looking down at Dave's fully clothed body. "Stand up." Dave did. "Now it's your turn," she said, her grin widening. "Strip."

Slightly embarrassed despite his high level of excitement, Dave removed his clothes, until he stood dressed only in his tight briefs, his erection barely contained.

"Show me that big hard cock of yours," Sherry said, and Dave pulled off his briefs. His cock stuck straight out—so swollen, it was painful.

Sherry reached out and ran her fingernails from base to oozing tip. "Nice. Are you ready to come for me?"

Dave didn't quite understand her choice of words. "Come for you?"

"I want to watch. Rub it."

Dave swallowed hard. No one had ever made this type of request of him. When he didn't immediately move, Sherry said, "I told you to do something. Didn't you hear me?"

"I heard."

"Good. I want you to rub some of the wonderful

sticky goo from my pussy all over your cock and make it spurt while I watch."

Dave hesitated, caught between raging lust and embarrassment. "I want to please you," he whispered.

Sherry suddenly understood. "This is the first time you've performed for an audience, isn't it?"

Dave swallowed again. "Yes."

Rather than being upset at his reluctance, Sherry smiled. "That's all right. I love virginal men." She took his hand. "Some incentive." She placed his hand between her legs. "Use my juices to wet that big cock of yours."

She rubbed Dave's fingers over her sopping pussy and then used his hand to spread her wetness onto his cock. "Now, show me, baby. Show me how hot I make you. Watch my tits and my pussy while you rub."

Dave watched Sherry's hands cup her breasts, pull at her nipples, and rub her crotch. Without really realizing what his hands were doing, he rubbed his cock until, with a roar, he spurted thick come onto the floor of the little room.

"Oh baby," Sherry purred. "You did so well."

Suddenly, there was a knock on the door and Tom's voice said, "Hey, Sherry, someone needs to see you up front."

Dave grabbed for his clothes and hurriedly dressed while Sherry calmly did the same.

"Can I help you?" the saleswoman said, dragging Dave back from his dream world. She had left the front counter and was now pushing a cartful of new books.

Dave glanced at her name tag. Sherry, it said. "I hope so," he said. "I certainly hope so."

HAL'S FANTASY

It was advertised as a boudoir gown and Harold had been staring at the ad in the magazine for several minutes. The gown was deep burgundy velvet, floor-length, with gold buttons from deep cleavage to thigh. The woman in the picture was gray-haired and quite mature-looking, but with a sexy, inviting gleam in her eyes. She was taking a step forward, so her beautiful leg, ending in a high-heeled burgundy mule trimmed with down, extended through the opening in the front.

The woman in the picture had a look in her eyes, as if she knew the secrets of every man she had ever been with. She understood a man's needs and desires and wanted nothing more than to fulfill them. God, Hal thought, closing his eyes. To be with such a woman.

"Good evening," she said as she opened the door.

"Hello, Michelle," Hal said. "Thank you for inviting me."

"When we met yesterday," the woman said, "I had the feeling that we could have a marvelous time together. Come in."

Hal walked into the apartment on the Left Bank. It was spring and all the windows were open to let in the soft Parisian air. The sounds of sidewalk vendors and children playing drifted into the sitting room. "Sit down," Michelle said, indicating an ivory brocade sofa. "Right here beside me."

Hal crossed the deeply carpeted floor and sat at the end of the sofa farthest from the woman. "I thought we might go out to eat," Hal said, now unsure as to why he had made this lunch date. He had met this enticing woman at a party thrown by a business associate the previous evening and had found her incredibly desirable.

"I thought we could stay in for lunch," she said, her voice low. "I've got a salade Niçoise and a wonderful bottle of white wine for us to share. But first, let's get to know each other a little bit. I gather you are in Paris on business."

For almost half an hour, the two talked, and gradually Hal relaxed. This was going to be all right. She was warm, funny, interested in his business, and quite knowledgeable about music and art. As they talked, she crossed her legs and the burgundy velvet she wore parted, allowing Hal a good look at her long legs. He cleared his throat and asked, "Have you lived here long?"

"I have been in this apartment for almost twenty years, since I sold my country home when my children grew up and moved away."

"You have children?" Hal didn't know why he was surprised, but he was.

"Oh, yes, I have three, all girls, all married. I am a grandmother six times."

She wasn't at all what he'd imagined the previous evening. He had actually thought she was trying to pick him up. He had thought she was a call girl. He smiled now at his silliness. She was a grandmother.

"That surprises you?" Michelle asked.

"I guess," Hal said.

"Ah," Michelle said. "You thought I was just a silly old woman, hungry for the company of a mature man like you." She laughed, a deep, throaty sound that made Hal think of naked breasts and parted thighs. "Well, in a way, you are right." She reached over, took his hand, and placed it on her knee. "I like men. It's as simple as that. I particularly like men with that look in their eyes that says, I want to make love to you."

"I never said that." Hal snatched his hand back.

"Yours words did not, but your eyes did. And they say that now when you look at me. I like that." Michelle took his hand and again placed it on her stocking-covered knee. "Wouldn't you like to be with me?"

Hal remained silent, unable to say yes but also unable to lie.

"Sit there and let me help you decide." She stood and walked around to the far side of the small coffee table. She placed her right foot on it, allowing her robe to part. "I like men to look at me," she said. She slid her hands up her thigh to the top of her stocking. She was wearing a black lace garter that she slowly stretched and pulled down to her knee, then down her calf to her burgundy mule. Delicately, she pulled her foot from her shoe and pulled the garter off over it. She leaned forward, took Hal's left hand, and put the garter around his wrist.

As she bent over, Hal could see her breasts, unconfined under her robe. Her flesh was white, her nipples smoky brown. He swallowed hard, unable to speak, knowing he wanted to touch those breasts more than he had ever wanted anything. He looked down at the garter around his wrist, then up into Michelle's deep blue eyes. Michelle put her foot back on the coffee table and slowly rolled the black stocking down her shapely leg, finally pulling it off so her red-painted toenails showed. She slipped her mule back on, then pulled the garter off her other leg the same way and placed it on the table. Then she rolled down her second stocking and placed it beside the first.

"You know," Michelle said as she walked around to sit beside Hal, "I very much like the way you look at me. Would you like to touch me?"

Again, Hal swallowed hard. "Yes," he whispered, unable to believe what was happening.

"Why don't you start by unbuttoning my robe?"

Hal grasped one tiny gold button and pushed it through the velvet loop that held it, then a second and a third. When the robe finally fell open, he gazed at Michelle's breasts, exposed above the wide black waist-cincher she wore. He had only glimpsed the loveliness of her breasts before. Now he saw them in their full glory. Neither large nor small, they were round, soft, and incredibly white. He extended his fingertips and brushed the silky flesh, so smooth and warm. He slid his fingers beneath them and lifted so they filled his hands.

"Do they please you?" she asked.

"Oh, they do," Hal groaned. "They are so beautiful."

"Would you like to kiss them?"

It was as though she knew what he wanted, what he needed, before he himself did. "Yes," he said, slowly lowering his head. He kissed first one globe, then the other, not yet trusting himself to touch or kiss her nipples. God he loved her breasts.

"Yes," she said. "Do what pleases you."

He buried his face in the valley between her breasts, inhaling her perfume, surrounding himself with the odor, the feel, the taste of her. He was in heaven, his body trembling with the need he was filled with.

Michelle leaned close to his ear. "We must please you," she said, her warm breath caressing his neck. She turned and slid forward until her hips were facing him, her body stretched on the sofa. Her bush was trimmed so that her pouting lips protruded, her flesh dewy and moist.

Hal, his face still pillowed between her breasts, felt her take one hand and guide it toward her inner thighs. "I think you would like to touch me," she whispered. "Explore my body. Know it well, so that when you enter me, it will be like entering an old friend who is new again."

"Oh Michelle," he purred. He sat back and used his fingers to get to know every crevice, every fold of her wetness.

"Touch me here," she said, guiding his finger to her clit. "Rub along and just to the side—slowly. Feel how hungry I get for you."

Glad to learn where and how this wonderful woman wanted to be touched, he rubbed where she showed him, watching her lips swell and her juices flow. He saw her eyes close and a small smile cross her face. "You make it hard to stop," she said softly, "but now I want to see you, too." When he hesitated, she said, "Please. Stand up and take off your clothes so we can touch, your skin against mine."

He stood, not knowing how he was going to disrobe in front of this woman he had known less than a day. He gazed into her eyes and saw her desire there. She wanted to look at him. He ran his fingers through his gray hair, then sighed and opened his light sport shirt. As he pulled it from his slacks and off of his shoulders, he saw Michelle smile. "You are very exciting to look at," she said softly. "Will you also take off your slacks for me?"

He could. A moment before he hadn't been sure, but now he was. Her eyes guided him. He opened his belt, unzipped his pants, and slid them and his shorts to the floor. Pulling off his shoes and socks in the same motion, he was suddenly naked, his penis semierect.

Michelle sat up and placed her palms against his belly. Slowly, she stroked first his chest, then his legs, then his buttocks. She placed her lips on the tip of his cock, then sucked it into her mouth. Then she released him and lay back on the sofa. "I don't want your cock too hard. I like it when a cock slides into me only a little hard. Then I can feel it grow and fill me."

She urged Hal to a position above her; then she used her fingers to place the tip of his cock against the entrance to her wet channel. Then she pushed it inside. She reached around and grabbed his cheeks, forcing his cock deeper inside. "Yes," she purred, "like that. Now as we love, I can feel you grow inside of me." She pulled his cheeks apart and fondled the flesh that only he had touched in the past.

Then she shifted her position and slipped one hand between his legs, cupping his balls, scratching them with her long fingernails. With her other hand, she lifted one breast so Hal's lips could suckle. "Oh, so good," she purred.

As she rubbed the sensitive skin between his testicles and his anus, he felt his cock harden. Slowly, he began to move inside of her, his mouth still sucking at her nipple.

"Rub me," she said, and she pressed his hand to the front of her mound. He easily found her clit. "Yes," she said, "like that."

As he moved, he rubbed her as she had shown him. "Yes," she said, her hands grabbing at his hips, pressing him hard against her. "Don't stop doing that." A moment later, she squeezed his flesh hard and said,

"Now don't move your hips. Hold very still and feel how my body needs this."

Although it was difficult, Hal stopped thrusting and rubbed Michelle's clit. Slowly, he felt her tighten, then felt waves of clenching muscles ripple along his cock. He felt her climax. He had never experienced anything like this before, but the sensation was almost irresistible. It was as if she were pulling him along into her orgasm.

He tensed, unable to hold still anymore. As if she had read his mind, she moved her hips and said, "Yes. Come with me."

He thrust only two or three times before he came, pumping his semen into her.

"Honey," his wife's voice said as she entered the bedroom. "I'm sorry. Were you asleep?"

"No," Hal said. "Just daydreaming."

"What's that you're reading?" She picked up the magazine and looked at the picture.

"I was actually thinking about getting that for you for your birthday," Hal said. "I think you'd look smashing." She would look so good in that robe!

Hal's wife grinned. "I'd look like a lady of the evening."

"Yes, you would," Hal said, grinning. "And what's wrong with that? That was just what I was dreaming about."

"Mmm. I like that thought." She looked back at the page. "How about we get the garters and stockings to go with it?"

"What a great idea," Hal said.